A Light Will Rise in Darkness

If you give yourself to the hungry,
and satisfy the desire of the afflicted,
then your light will rise in darkness
and your gloom will become like mid-day.

—Isaiah: 58:10

D0088564

A Light Will Rise in Darkness

Growing Up Black and Catholic in New Orleans

Jo Anne Tardy

A Light Will Rise in Darkness
Growing Up Black and Catholic in New Orleans
by Jo Anne Tardy

Edited by Gregory F. Augustine Pierce
Cover design by Tom A. Wright
Cover art "Reflections on Bourbon Street" by M.P. Wiggins, TheSpiritsource.com
Typesetting by Desktop Edit Shop, Inc.

Published by   ACTA Publications
                Assisting Christians To Act
                5559 W. Howard Street
                Skokie, IL 60077-2621
                800-397-2282
                www.actapublications.com

Library of Congress Catalog number: 2006931877

ISBN 10: 0-87946-316-3
ISBN 13: 978-0-87946-316-8

Printed in the United States of America

Year 12 11 10 09 08 07 06
Printing 10 9 8 7 6 5 4 3 2 1

Contents

Dedication

To the Almighty Father
To my beloved Adonai, Jesus
To the Holy Spirit
To Saint Katherine Drexel
To Blessed Henriette Delille, SSF
To Sister Mary Colombiere, SBS
To Sister Mary Gerald, DC
To Dr. Joanne Caldwell
To the Colla, Green, Lombard and Tardy Families
To my spouse, Melvin Tardy, Sr.
To my children Pamela Branson, Melvin Tardy, Jr., and Gregory Tardy
To Charlie Branson, Annie Tardy and Janel Tardy
To my grandchildren Antonio, Trevor, Martell,
Lily Rose, Sarah, Isaac,
Gabriel and Abigail
To my mother Margery

And to all those whose times denied them the luxury of literacy
yet who entrusted their lives and stories to a little girl
who would remember and eventually record in this book
their eloquent existences and noble contributions
as humble servants of God

A Note from the Publisher

Black. Catholic. New Orleans. How could we not include in "The American Catholic Experience" Jo Anne Tardy's reminiscences of growing up in the Big Easy, especially after the destruction wrought by Hurricane Katrina and its aftermath? This is exactly what we want this series to be: first-person reflections by laypeople on the wide variety of individual experiences of lived Catholicism in the United States, and certainly Tardy's book makes a real contribution.

This is a beautifully written book that captures a unique place and time in the great American and great Catholic experiments in diversity. We cannot have a real picture of American Catholicism without the story of "growing up black and Catholic in New Orleans," just as we cannot have it without the story of growing up Polish and Catholic in Chicago or Irish and Catholic in Boston or Native American and Catholic in South Dakota or Latino and Catholic in San Antonio or Asian and Catholic in San Francisco. So we will continue to publish books in this series until we have the complete mosaic of the American Catholic Experience.

But why should *you* read this book and the others in the series? Read them to discover what the church (small c) in the United States is really like. Not from the top down, but from the bottom up. Read them to learn why American Catholics love their faith and stick with their church (small c and large C) even when it disappoints them. Read them to hear the voice of laypeople, unencumbered by the theological expectations or orthodoxy concerns of the church (large C). Most of all, read them because they are just good, interesting, stories about what it is like to be a Catholic in the United States in the last half of the twentieth and the first part of the twenty-first centuries.

Jo Anne Tardy has been a teacher, a dancer, a songwriter, an opera and a jazz singer, a wife and mother. She has lived in Indianapolis, Milwaukee and St. Louis, and she is presently retired and living with her husband Melvin in Stockton, California. But her story begins in the Algiers section of New Orleans in the 1940s and 1950s, where she was born and spent her childhood. This is the story of *A Light Will Rise in Darkness*. Let her tell you about her grandfather, Manuel, her grandmother, Jenny, her mother, Margery, her numerous aunts and uncles and cousins and friends. And about her father, an African prince whom she never met.

Let her also talk about what it meant to her to be Catholic and black (or "colored" as she calls it) in New Orleans back then.

So lean back, pour yourself a mint julep or a cup of chicory coffee, and enjoy a trip back to the New Orleans and the Catholicism that existed before Katrina, before the Superdome, before Vatican II. Learn how a young girl discovered how her light could rise in darkness.

Gregory F. Augustine Pierce
President and Co-Publisher
ACTA Publications

Foreword

by Reverend Theodore Hesburgh, C.S.C.
President Emeritus, University of Notre Dame

A merican Catholicism is a patchwork quilt. From the early immigrants from western and eastern Europe to the more recent immigrants from Latin America, Asia and Africa, American Catholics have worked to make this a great church in a great country, without abandoning their affection for and affinity to their native lands and churches.

Two unique patches of that quilt are black Catholics and the Catholics of New Orleans. I have been fortunate to spend much of my life's work at the University of Notre Dame. Although now heavily identified with the Irish, Notre Dame was actually founded by a native of France, Fr. Edward Sorin, C.S.C. New Orleans, of course, was touched by the French culture more than most cities in the United States. This in combination with other cultures led to a unique kind of Catholicism that reflected the particular "Cajun" blend of beliefs and practices. And the black Catholic experience has also been different, partly because of the experience of slavery and the historical reality of racism in the Catholic church, and partly because of the contemporary strength of identification of blacks with our Christian friends and brethren in some Protestant denominations, such as the Baptists and the Methodists.

So to read *A Light Will Rise in Darkness* by Jo Anne Tardy was a revelation to me. Here was an African American cradle Catholic, born and raised in the Algiers section of New Orleans, who had remained strong in her faith despite difficult life challenges, and she was also the daughter of a real African prince. More than her unique background, however, makes this a special book. Jo Anne Tardy is a free spirit, one who took the divine life that was given to her and developed it in every way she could. We Catholics call that process incarnation.

She also has a gift for writing, able to allow us to smell what she smelled, see what she saw, hear what she heard, taste what she tasted, and touch what she touched. What she has described here is the city of New Orleans and the Catholicism of her youth. After reading this book, I feel that I know New Orleans Catholicism of the 1940s and 1950s, and it was a beautiful thing. I identify with the priests of her parish and the nuns of her schools and her grandparents and mother and aunts and uncles and cousins and friends, who were stalwarts of the New Orleans church.

And then there is Jo Anne herself. I have met her through her son, Mel, who I'm proud to say is a graduate and employee of Notre Dame. It was a chance meeting at our Grotto on campus during Mel's commencement weekend. But it is one thing to meet a colleague's mom before a university function and quite another to meet her first as a little girl, then as a teenager, a college student, a young woman, and a wife and mother. This is the Jo Anne Tardy I met in the pages of this book, and I encourage you to make her acquaintance as well.

I want to say one more word about the series of which her story is a part. There is little first-person material written by U.S. Catholic laypeople about their experience of connecting their faith with their daily life, and it is a pleasure to see *The American Catholic Experience* being published by ACTA Publications. These are books that students of Catholicism at Notre Dame and in schools around the country should read before they graduate if they want to understand the Catholicism that has shaped the generations before them and the country in which they live. I am proud to place copies of each book of this series in the university library, and I have been assured that the publisher will continue to do so until every segment of the quilt that is American Catholicism has had a chance to tell its story.

Introduction

When it became apparent that Hurricane Katrina would definitely hit New Orleans, the city of my birth and of my life for the first thirty-seven years, I decided to speak with God before I went to bed that night. I reminded Him of all the good, praying people who "lived" in the Algiers section where I grew up.

These people, truly holy during their lives and exemplars to me, now rested in the cemeteries of Algiers. I asked God for just one favor: "Please, God, protect my mother's bones, those of my grandfather, my grandmother, my uncles and aunts, and especially those of my Aunt Aline. Let them not be disturbed by this storm, for they were peace-makers during their lives and their footprints mark the streets of Algiers." I then went to sleep, safe in my Stockton, California, bed.

The next day I watched in horror the televised scenes of my home city's unspeakable disintegration. Between tears and sobs, I strained to recognize a familiar face while wondering which of my friends, former co-workers, former students were dead or alive. My heart hung low in utter pain as I considered that I had just recorded in detail in this very book the way New Orleans was as I grew up there. My passion for this unique, historic city had stirred me to write music, including my recorded song "City of the River," and now this book.

Hearing Aaron Neville's beautiful voice, just seeing him on television, comforted me with hope that the city and state would be resilient. I know Aaron Neville and of his great devotion to St. Jude, the Saint of the Impossible. And I know the spirit of the people of New Orleans, who have time and again come through many tragedies that defy logic.

It surprised me a couple of weeks later to learn that my brother, who had initially evacuated to Baton Rouge, was back living in his Algiers home. He told me that Algiers had been spared—despite news reports to the contrary. "Our levee never broke!" he told me. Then my heart leapt for joy. My God had not disappointed me. Algiers had been "sheltered," the very word I had used in this book to describe it.

The full tragedy of Katrina is now evident. But New Orleans has survived and is beginning to rebuild. A light will rise in darkness, just as the Scripture promises. And so I can share with you my experience of growing up black and Catholic in New Orleans.

Manuel the Healer

Always in pain, most times they made appointments. Sometimes they just showed up with canes, crutches or casts, but they left improved, looking relieved. Apparently, Grandpa had the gift.

Mystified, I would peer from the doorway of the dining room, the distance of a room away, watching another ailing human sitting in our house before Grandpa, explaining a problem to him with all the confidence in the world. What on earth did this mean to a little girl? But this happened all the time, as early as I can remember.

Whenever anyone suffering did come by, Grandpa stopped whatever he was doing, listened to the seeker, blessed himself, often kneeling on one knee as if in meditation, then began to massage the troubled area prayerfully. On more than one occasion, I noted this usual though unusual transpiration: Grandpa appeared to be making the sign of the cross three times while touching the afflicted area, and he would barely audibly utter something that sounded like: *"A Te in Sacri Uncte."*

Out of deep respect for Grandpa, no one ever questioned him nor ever even talked about his healing power. It was just accepted as part of the natural order of things. No one knew how to ask him what he did, what he said, or how this all worked. But everyone who knew my maternal grandfather was aware that, from time to time, people went to 1232 Vallette Street in New Orleans to be touched by him. They all came to be touched by a special man. I won't claim miracles, since nobody in the house talked about it. Likewise, I can't say miracles didn't happen, because I was not told that they didn't. But it seemed to me, a young girl who was both credulous and skeptical at the same time, that people who had been ill or ailing appeared to recover within days of being touched and prayed for by Grandpa. I am sure that he enjoyed singular respect from both the black and the white communities of the city. Everyone I knew trusted Manuel Placide Lombard.

Grandpa could often be seen on his knees, praying alone in his room after any of these suppliants left his home. None of his children or grandchildren would bother him when he was praying. Still, none of us thought it unusual for him to pray, for he rarely passed his church without going inside to pray alone, often leaving his untethered horse and wagon outside, which would always be there when he returned. If he was driving and could not go inside, he would at least tip his cap in acknowledgement of the Source of his faith and power.

Why was my grandfather so respected by other people?

Grandpa never took money or anything from the people who came to ask him to help them get well. Although at the time I was not quite understanding and half disbelieving what I witnessed, I always saw them smile and gratefully say, "Thank you."

I just wondered how this all came to be: This was my grandfather, an everyday good man, the one who raised me, fed me. Why was my grandfather so respected by other people?

Many years later, at my grandfather's funeral, I would hear a priest relate to a thronged church how he, as a nervous young assistant pastor, had been assigned to Algiers Parish not knowing what to expect, but he had been advised by past pastors of All Saints Church to: "Get in touch with Manuel Lombard. He'll tell you all you need to know." I heard him say on the altar that my grandfather was a true saint.

Grandpa was a man who kept pace with the sun. In order to do this, he had to wake up within the darkness that preceded it. One can only wonder at the private thoughts and conversations he must have had with nature, but one curious person did attempt to learn one time.

"Grandpa, could you wake me up when you wake up tomorrow morning?" I asked. "I want to see the sun rise." Grandpa seemed happy to comply with my request. I could tell by the unusual smile in his eyes. I could also tell that tomorrow was going to be special. So I happily went to bed that night really early. The whole household was quite surprised! Everyone knew I always tried to find excuses to stay up way past my bedtime. They all wondered what had possessed me now, but I determined to go to bed early this one night.

I hoped my grandfather would not forget to wake me, but I need not have worried. Grandpa never made a promise he did not keep. For once, I forgot about the boogeymen I feared in the dark, whose eyes I once thought I saw coming to life on the knobs and whorls of wood on the bedroom furniture. Tonight this little girl was going to sleep happy, happy, happy! And I was, indeed, soon off to an excitedly peaceful slumber.

The next thing I heard was the sound of a strong, familiar, but gentle voice announcing, "Jo Anne, it's time to wake up." I saw that the room was still dark—dark as night. The kerosene lamp was still lit on the mantelpiece to help still my only slightly harbored fear of the dark. I could also see the electric light on in the kitchen. Blissful that Grandpa remembered to wake me, I put on my robe and slippers quietly so as not to wake anyone else. This was to be our special adventure.

The two of us walked into the kitchen where we could talk unheard.

"Is this morning?" I asked.

"Yes, the sun will be up in just a few minutes," Grandpa answered. I think he wanted me to be wide awake for this special event. "Here, drink you some tea," he offered. He had fixed a tiny glass of warm tea and milk for me. I enjoyed his attention like nothing else I had ever experienced.

The world seemed quiet, a different kind of quiet than normal quiet. Almost everyone else was asleep. I had figured early on that I might have my grandfather all to myself for a change, without having to share him with everyone else, but I hadn't realized how quiet it would be. I sipped some of the warm tea.

"Jo Anne, come see!" he said.

As we walked out to the enclosed back porch, through the screened door, down the steps, a most beautiful sight began to reveal itself across the sky. An exquisite, glowing mantle of rose color was gracefully lifting itself and nudging away the purpled black darkness. Our backyard had a mystical blue tint, and a glimmering yellow danced along the lower edge of the rosy mantle hem. Everything in the backyard seemed to be magically transforming from blue to pink. Within minutes, the sun thrust up its own yellow brilliance, authoritatively pushing away what was left of the night.

"Grandpa, it's so beautiful," I said. "Do you see this every morning?"

Birds began chirping happily all around the yard. It became a wonderland few young girls experience. Grandpa must have noted how taken I was with all this beauty.

He took me by the hand and helped me back up the steps and inside the screened door. I ran inside and told Grandma how pretty the sunrise was. But, of course, she already knew. She fixed me some hot French bread and butter while Grandpa tended to the horses.

Though I have forgotten many things about my childhood, I'll remember that morning forever.

The House on Vallette Street

Not too long ago, in a little section of New Orleans sheltered by the crescent of the levee of the Mississippi River, lived a little town called Algiers. Algiers was many things to many people—feared by some because of its rumored voodoo practices, sought by others for its exotically beautiful mulatto women, but to the Lombard family it was home.

The Lombard house was a modest white double shotgun. Royal maroon trimmed the screened windows to match the darkly gleaming wooden front doors. Like so many New Orleans homes it was built high above ground, with no basement, for protection against floods that might occur during hurricane season or after any very hard rain. Stained glass windows peered undisturbed from the anterior of the high attic. One front door was never opened, except on steamy summer nights to invite complaisant air to gently waltz through the gauzily curtained screen. The front porch was of strong wood, and concrete steps framed by symmetrical sets of gracefully sloping stoops led down from each of the two doors to the sidewalk.

On the stoop in front of the door forbidden to human traffic, wandering jew—dewy, green and purple—grew for years in a creamy oval metal container. The other stoops were free for sitting. The façade was bolstered by three huge white stone pillars that became sturdy white wood upon their ascent to the ceiling of the porch.

Tempting Japonica trees flirted over the alley gate, while a tall oak stood guard near the street edge of the frontage. One chinaberry quivered its tiny balls onto the grass, as if in competition with the tasty fruit of the Japonicas. Pink, red and white roses managed to grow all around the house. The rear of the property offered fresh pale mirletons for cooking, as well as pumpkins that ripened around Halloween back by the coal shed. Most conveniently for my grandfather, Manuel Placide Lombard, a red pepper plant grew next to the back steps of the house where he could pick a fresh pepper to crush into his evening dinner anytime he wished.

A red pepper plant grew next to the back steps of the house where he could pick a fresh pepper to crush into his evening dinner anytime he wished.

A profusion of lilacs, azaleas, four o'clocks and sweet, sweet honeysuckles bloomed just about everywhere. And the night-blooming jasmines caressed the house. They grew tall to lend privacy to the many love affairs that blossomed over the years on the front porch.

Still within the frontage at 1232 Vallette Street was a lovingly tended garden with a variety of ferns, irises, gladiolas, gardenias and calla lilies that would bloom during the latter part of the Lenten season. One St. Joseph Lily would perennially bloom without fail for Holy Thursday. It would find itself placed on an altar at All Saints Catholic Church not many blocks away, always in time for Holy Week festivities.

Directly across the street from the Lombard residence was St. Bartholomew's, the immaculate white cemetery now the resting home of at least a century of former Algerians. No one in our house ever had a problem with our permanently sleeping neighbors. That is, no one ever claimed outright to have seen a ghost on Vallette Street. On the contrary, it seemed a quite peaceful, pretty, safe and pleasant place for a nice, quiet walk. Besides the ever-sweet smell of freshly mown green grass there, one could admire the array of high, majestic, ornate stone and marble structures with their elegantly sculptured angels, miniature white or black wrought iron fences, and tiny pieces of crystal white granite pebbles that covered some of the crypts of modest height.

A huge alabaster crucifix, about evenly centered directly across from Manuel Lombard's house, seemed to keep vigil for the people of Algiers. Each row of graves housing their unseen tenants brought pleasure to the eye of the beholder. The structures were as meticulously aesthetic as anything one might view in an art museum. There was absolutely nothing eerie nor frightening about living across the street from this beautiful place, although I must admit that some occurrences there were always difficult to explain.

Manuel Lombard and Honore Landrieu were next-door neighbors. Each owned businesses and struggled to support themselves and their extended families. Their trades complemented each other's, and the two men were friends. Each had a French heritage. Honore was French on both sides, that is, both his parents were pure Acadian. Although Manuel's maternal grandfather had come from France, someone on his father's side had married a person of color. Thus, by law of Louisiana and despite their Caucasian appearance, Manuel and each of his seven brothers and sisters were called Negroes.

This was difficult for some in my family, who in time migrated to other parts of the United States and took to "passing" for what they looked like—white—in hope of a better life. The rest of us stayed home in New Orleans, and this story is about us.

Manuel was the Ice Man of Algiers. This appellation had nothing to do with his temperament. Early before each sunrise, he would awake, say his morning prayers, put on his starched khaki uniform, kiss his wife Jenny goodbye, drink a hot glass of freshly brewed tea with milk, and eat buttery toast Jenny would fix him. After scanning the front page of the morning paper, he would mention a few items of interest. The two would talk about the obligations of the day, their eight children, and their one granddaughter—me. Then, after brushing his strong, tanned, weathered fingers through his curly black locks twice, Manuel would don his cap, pocket his order booklet, go out the back door, and brush past the dew-laden leaves of the fragrant but barren orange tree to ready the horses.

About this time, the chickens would be up and around, some cautiously stepping over warm, newly-laid brown and white eggs. Others were cackling and fussing about their offspring and about the big fiery-necked rooster trumpeting his cock-a-doodle-doos for attention and strutting around like he owned the place after trying to have his way with them. Improvisation and instinct had apparently designed their unique lodging arrangements for the night, because a strange early morning ritual would reveal most of them at various points atop the roof of the back shed and on the limbs of the big shade tree. The previous evening, they would have one by one urged their plump, feathered bodies upward, flapping their wings for all they were worth until each had secured its own favorite roost. These motley-colored creatures looked like over-sized ornaments decorating a Christmas tree.

The ice wagon needed only one horse. Its cab, white at top and sides, hailed in bright-red capital letters: LOMBARD ICE. The bottom section of the cab was a brownish green. The driver's seat could hold two adults, but if a lucky child were small enough, she might manage to be squeezed in for a ride with her grandfather and his helper.

The Ice Man Cometh

roudly, Manuel P. Lombard strode across his huge yard to his stable, which sheltered three horses: Paint, Nelly, and Black Beauty. Nelly was an older horse, white in color. Remembering her past service, Manuel gently pat her on the nose as she whinnied good morning, aware that she could rest at will on her sweet bed of hay. Manuel looked over at Black Beauty, a new acquisition, an exquisite mare but high strung and not yet accustomed to hard work. She would do in time. "Here now! Here now!" he'd exclaim as he'd gently, but firmly, lead the stallion Paint out of the stable. "Okay, boy. You and I have some work to do today."

Manuel loved his horses; they loved him. Man and beast were both aware that each possessed power, strength and history. Yet, in a sort of respectful agreement, the two cooperated, seemingly cognizant that fate had placed them together and each depended on the other for survival. The horses instinctively trusted Manuel. He was that breed of human that animals love.

In earlier days, Paint had been a racehorse. His strong, dark brown body was still handsome, and his pride emanated from the lustrous black-brown mane trailing down his highly poised head and neck. Aware, haughty eyes seemed to illuminate the splash of white down the center of his face that gave him his name.

In another place and time, Paint and Manuel might have been

friends. But in the 1940s, Manuel had responsibilities. And Manuel was in charge. Somewhat reconciled to obeying, Paint allowed Manuel to bridle him and back him into position to be hitched to the wagon with little resistance. He knew the routine. Once the leather controls were in place, Manuel would quietly lead him and the wagon on foot so as not to wake the children and granddaughter as they slept oblivious to his cares for the day, and so as not to awaken Emma, who lived in a little one-room shack right next to the front gate of the Lombard property.

Manuel worried about Emma. She was his eldest sister, whom no one had taken in marriage. She had been engaged once, but somehow her betrothed became more captivated by her younger sister Alma. What a family predicament that must have been! Nevertheless, Manuel had handled it just as his father would have wanted him to: "Manuel, you're the oldest boy. You're smart. Promise me you'll keep the family together and take care of your mother Louise for me." His father had exacted this pledge as he lay dying, poisoned by a deranged sister.

Manuel wished he could have remained in school. He had been an apt student through the fifth grade and would definitely miss his friends. Yet his mother had just given birth to his baby sister Rita a short time before, and now the actions of his aunt, whom everyone knew should have been locked up years before, had altered my grandfather's dreams for the future.

Great-grandfather had just begun giving Manuel violin lessons. How Manuel loved to play the violin. His teacher had noticed his wonderful talent, great hands, and natural ear for the instrument. But how would his mother, brothers and sisters live now if Manuel didn't bring food into the house? These violinist hands and studious mind must prematurely seek sustenance for his family—George, Leon, Louis,

Lucien, Emma, Alma, Rita and their Mama. Little Manuel would have to take care of them all.

At his father's funeral Manuel wanted to cry, but he felt he mustn't. "I had to show my brothers and sisters that we all need to be strong," he told me years later. "I had to set the example. I had to be the man. I had to be a father to my sisters and brothers." He promised his mother, "Don't cry, Mama, and don't worry. I'll take care of you and everybody."

Looking towards her back door as he passed by each morning, Manuel realized that Emma was lucky to even be alive.

Manuel worked every job he could secure. Early on he found work on the other side of the river at Kolb's, a well-known restaurant. He supplemented this work as a dock hand at the ferry boat. He made enough to keep red beans, rice and French bread on the table, with fried catfish on Fridays and a roast chicken on Sundays.

Over the years, each of Manuel's siblings married suitably, except for Emma. Looking towards her back door as he passed by each morning, Manuel realized that Emma was lucky to even be alive. When she was born, the doctor had told his mother that her baby girl would not last through the night and had given her a shoebox in which to bury her the next morning.

It was usual for babies to be delivered at home in those days, and an informal burial of stillborns was a common practice. A week later, however, the doctor returned to check on the condition of Manuel's mother only to be astounded at healthy cries of an infant who had not died after all. All this information had been relayed to Manuel, because he had not yet been born. Emma was the oldest child in the family. Manuel was the second-born, and they had six younger brothers and sisters.

Manuel recognized Emma had no one else to be concerned for her, so he allowed her to live on his property but in a separate house, where he could keep an eye on her, where she could have some privacy, and where she might not cause too much friction between him and his wife.

By the time Manuel unlocked the big unpainted wooden gate and securely parked the horse and wagon outside to relock it each morning, his neighbor Honore Landrieu was sweeping the sidewalk in front of his grocery store, taking care round the sides of the big wood breadbox that sat over to one side beneath the large picture window.

"Hoo dere, Mr. Manuel, how you dis mawnin'?" Honore would ask.

"Hey there, Mr. Noree'! Everything's awright?" Grandpa would ask.

"Sho' look like we gon' have a hot one today. *Picayune* say it gon' get up to ninety-four degrees. Well, I guess dat's good for de ice business."

"I hope so anyway," Grandpa agreed. "You ought to sell a few root beers today too." Both men chuckled, as only lifelong friends can.

Manuel mounted the driver's seat and yelled, "Giddy up," giving Paint a slight lick on the rump with the reins. He headed down Vallette Street towards the Rantz Ice Factory to pick up his day's supplies.

Clop, clop, clop, clop, clop, clop, clop, clop, clop beat Paint's hooves against the humid Algiers streets in syncopation with the constant whir of the iron wheels of the ice wagon as it rolled over the smoothed-down blue-grey cobbled stones. Paint knew the route to the ice factory. He was familiar with the sounds and smells along the way. A grey poodle yipped from between the black laced iron rails of the porch of the two-story brick house on the corner as Paint and Manuel made a left turn past a little white clapboard flower shop before continuing between the two cemeteries—St. Bartholomew's on the left and St. Mary's on the right. "Fewer people to disturb if we take this route," thought Manuel. He made a right along the rear of the St. Mary's Cemetery.

Looking to his left, he saw Miss Ritah, an extremely light-skinned

Creole widow walking in the opposite direction on her way to morning Mass, as was her custom.

"Hello, Mr. Manuel, fifty pounds today," she said as she flashed a friendly smile.

"All right, Miz Ritah, catch you on my way back."

Manuel continued on his way, but he thought, "Hmm! Miz Ritah usually orders twenty-five." He calculated mentally: "I suppose I'd better pick up extra today. Probable double business if this heat keeps up the way it's going." And he began to think about the snowball stands starting up business in humid days like this. There would definitely be more of a demand for ice today.

A few blocks down, Manuel passed the beer garden. The fresh warm early morning air began to reek of stale spilt beer from the previous night. A man who had imbibed too many to make it home was sprawled out on the sidewalk in deep slumber. Broken pieces of green and brown bottle glass poked out of the grass, curving down and out to the street, exhibiting evidence of the carousing that usually transpired on this block. Carefully, Manuel eyed the street to be certain nothing would trip or cut Paint.

The faint sound of some cursing between an unseen man and a woman reached earshot. But this was not unusual for this block. Anything could happen here, and there was nothing Manuel could do about it anyway, except to go on about his business.

The next block resumed the air of early-morning quiet, except for the meow of a yellow tabby cat that suddenly decided to dart from behind some azaleas to run across the street into an alley. Two sailors were walking in the direction of the Algiers Ferry. They probably would have to wait for the next boat, because the captain was already signaling the warning whistle for take off. The loud whoo whoot could be heard all over Algiers.

The sight of the sailors made Manuel think again about his oldest son, James. He had been at once proud and fearful the day James had left for the Army. James was a handsome, fine son—enough to make any man proud. And as a man who had performed his own tour of duty during an earlier war, Manuel knew it was every man's patriotic responsibility to do what he could to protect the country. He had raised James well and knew he would make a good soldier, but this was turning out to be a most horrible war—with Hitler, Mussolini and Hirohito all trying to take over the world.

Manuel missed James. Big, strong James. This dutiful son would help him in mornings and evenings with the heavy work. The way everyone talked about how strong James was, you'd think he was Samson. Well, it did seem superhuman the way he'd single-handedly carried that big iron safe with all the parish money in it out of the burning school that time. Where on earth had he gotten that strength? Because after he'd brought the safe out of the building, he couldn't pick it up again. It took four guys to even budge it. Anyway, after that incident, everyone called his son "Big James."

Surely God had taken care of James that time to do His work. Hopefully, He'd bring James back home again after he'd complete what needed to be done over there.

A left turn towards the levee and straight down to the dead end put Manuel in front of the Rantz Ice Factory. You could faintly hear the machinery from the street. Paint knew what to do. "Whoa!" Paint obeyed to a full stop. He knew Manuel would want him to back up and turn. Although the horse couldn't see behind him, he recognized the familiar sounds. Manuel had to position him so as to back the cab of the wagon flush with the wooden dock of the factory. He secured Paint and the wagon to an iron post and then walked up the steps and along the dock to the door of the factory.

Opening the door unleashed an almost deafening roar of machinery and a blast of Nordic air. Huge slabs of one-hundred-pound ice rectangles glided across the floor in iron missiles. The two men could barely hear as they shouted morning pleasantries to each other, but Mr. Rantz respected Mr. Lombard—they were two ice men in business together. Both were tall. Both hard-working. And both rose before the sun while everyone else slept. Rantz anticipated what Manuel would need. They had been doing business together for so long, one manufacturing and the other delivering ice to people who needed it.

Like all good businessmen, Rantz and Lombard were sensitive to the needs of their customers. They both tended the perennial cooling needs of the humid Algerians. It was a rewarding enterprise for two essential gentlemen of the South, and it helped make the world a better place, a little more like the way God would have things.

Jo Anne at age four.

Funeral Parades
and Flooded Canals

L amarque Street was cut off at Vallette Street by a little brick buttress intended to shield people from the murky canal below the street. But from this little aqueduct, people liked to rest and look down at the water. No matter how dark, it somehow soothed. The bridge was about waist high on an adult, and it had a little long narrow step on which I liked to sit as a child while the big people took time for a chat. Once in a while, someone would pick me up so I could look down at the water.

Lamarque and Vallette was a very peaceful corner because no traffic could pass through the Lamarque Street Canal, which stretched back to Lower Algiers. This little structure, this little spot at the canal, seemed an anchoring haven to me. Anyone could stop and rest there and talk to anyone. As well, anyone could just rest there and look.

What would they look at? Well, usually nothing special, nothing really out of the ordinary that couldn't be seen every day. Permanent sights at this corner were the sparkling white E. J. Mothe Funeral Home, which resembled a sprawling plantation occupying the entire thirteenth block of Vallette Street. On the other side of the canal, the white clapboard Baptist Church, with its baptismal area and green open lot spread out behind it.

Diagonally across from the church stood the faded wooden home of its chief overseer, a tall, strong, proud black woman with a most prominent lower lip. She was called Tootie Payton. Across the street from her house was the edge of the St. Bartholomew Cemetery.

Lamarque and Vallette was usually a calm, very quiet corner, unless you count the times Miss Payton, eyes blazing, would run outside across the street to shoo away hapless little Catholic children who chanced to play on the unfenced empty church back lot.

"No Catholics on Baptist property," she would yell. "Get on away from here!"

"Jo Anne, let's run!" my friends would shout. "Here come the big lip lady!"

This block did have a special treat, but it could only happen when somebody died. Thomp, thomp, thadomp! Thomp, thomp, thadomp! I could feel the big bass drum's hypnotic summons from way beyond the other end of the block. Someone would yell, "A funeral parade" and everyone would drop whatever he or she was doing to run outside. This wouldn't happen every day, but on rare weeks it happened more than once.

Strangely, I cannot explain the intense feeling that overtook me whenever I heard that mournful dirge nearing. The bass drum's pensive, pounding pulse penetrated my heart, scaring me. Yet the music fascinated me. A clarinet would squeal its dulcet, impassioned sorrow. The honeyed, visceral vibrato of the slide trombone seemed to curl its way around my heart to console and comfort me. The tuba echoed purifying profundity. I would run to the front porch when the drumbeat called and watch the parade of musicians dressed in black and white. Some wore assorted black caps and hats, and a few wore banners with gold fringes. I watched, but I tried to shield my eyes from the hearse. I knew a dead man was inside.

I was both intrigued and appalled.

Throngs always gathered in the streets as a funeral entered the Baptist church on the corner. They would wait in the hot sun with handkerchiefs, wiping cascades of sweat from their faces. Some would wait leaning against a tree across the street. Others straddled their bicycles, feet resting on the ground. I had a ringside seat on my front porch.

When the service was very long, however, the musicians became demystified. They felt the effects of the smothering Algiers heat just like everyone else.

Everyone knew that eventually the most stirringly jubilant jazz parade would emerge from that church. A second line would be dancing. And all traffic would stop.

It didn't matter what color or religion you were, you could watch. Though it took me years to understand why all the tears of sorrow that entered that edifice were transformed into such joy on the way out, as a child, it appeared to me that everyone was suddenly happy that the person was dead. That did puzzle me. But the joy was palpable.

When the service was very long, however, the musicians became demystified. They felt the effects of the smothering Algiers heat just like everyone else. They came outside to cool off, bought a cool soft drink from the grocery, and walked down by our house to sit on our steps and drink it while sharing a conversation with my grandfather if he was home. Our big shade tree in front of the house seemed a haven from the sun.

People were seeking temporary relief from the blazing illumination, both from the sun and from the funeral, and my family had it. Sometimes people would ask me to go inside to fetch them a cold glass of water, and I would accommodate them, as they all seemed to know my grandfather. Sometimes they would talk about the dead man, who he was, how he'd died and all. Early on, I don't recall the jazz bands being used for women. In fact, I distinctly remember the absence of jazz bands at women's funerals.

Sometimes the conversations included topics not so morbid. I got to know some of the musicians this way. I remember in particular Mr. Peter Bocage and Mr. Freddie Kohlman. It was also a fact that my grandfather was in position to hire musicians for other types of occasions. Grandpa was someone who just made things happen, and he was admired for that.

By and by, when the church service was nearly over, someone would send for the jazz musicians. Now the parade would march back into the direction from which it had come, picking up extra marchers dancing with umbrellas and white handkerchiefs, passing our house. I would watch and listen as long as I could see anything from my porch until all the excitement had left me behind. Then I'd go back into the house, feeling somewhat melancholy and not knowing why. Perhaps the music had emphasized an empty silence in my own life. It was too quiet now.

I usually filled this quiet with my thoughts, my wonderings, my daydreams, my mental lists of things I loved in my own little world. Sometimes I wondered what my adult life would be like, and often I thought about some aspect of music. Sometimes I wished for rain. I enjoyed raindrops—gentle raindrops, heavy raindrops—but the rain sounded like music. It made different tones on everything it touched. The old rusty barrel in the yard sounded like a drum. Poinsettia leaves sounded as if they were being tapped by a drummer's brushes. Rain through the trees sounded like echoes of muffled choral voices. Rain on the roof, according to its intensity, sounded like gentle plucking of guitar strings or like piano keystrokes.

Huge rainstorms would sometimes cause the canal at the corner of

Vallette and Lamarque to flood up, almost like a lake. The rising waters would stretch far beyond the corner and the flooded canal transformed the scene of quiet rest to one of merriment. Young people from all around Algiers donned bathing suits if they had them, or just shorts or cut-off pants if they did not, and splashed into the water to enjoy this unexpected bounty from the sky.

One time a small boy came rolling a dusty black tire and placed it gingerly into the water. He lifted himself onto the tire and savored the gentle float along the length of the now gleaming dark canal. He stopped when the current got too close to the underside of the canal bridge. He jumped off, pulled himself up the embankment, walked his little muddy feet across the green wet grass until he found a spot where he could climb back down to the water and repeat the process.

Some children put pale wooden Popsicle sticks into little folded pieces of paper to fashion a boat. They tried to see how far they could watch their creation float down the canal before the current would take it beyond where any eye could see it and sail into the mysterious dark tunnel that went under the bridge and towards the levee that cradled the west bank of the mighty Mississippi River.

But the Lombard children were not permitted to indulge this water. We could just stand and watch—and not too closely. My grandfather was so protective. He feared we might drown, and probably rightly so. There were no lifeguards, no safeguards he could see that would not stop anyone who decided to walk or slide down the side of the embankment. We were forbidden to enter the water, and that was that.

We wondered what it might have been like to participate. Other people seemed to be having so much fun. Standing there on the corner, I asked my mother over and over why could I not go down to the canal. She told me there might be snakes in the water. I asked her why other children's mothers let them play in the canal, but I was informed that I was not an other person's child. I was her only child. Mama also made certain her younger siblings did not approach too closely the water's edge. She warned us that within a week all the children in the canal would become infested with boils and sores from germs and other unknown things. No sooner had she said this than a scream rang out!

A teenaged girl running up the banks screamed, "A lampeel! A lampeel!" Other bathers scurried out of the water screaming too. There was much confused commotion, seeming to confirm what my mother had predicted. Momentarily, a large boy climbed out of the water with what looked like a long, dead snake and proclaimed loudly, "It's okay. I killed it!" People excitedly gathered around the hero to look at it. My mother, always the teacher, told me that the girl had been trying to say that the creature was a lamprey. Mama then called the hero over to where we were standing so I could see it. He happily obliged, proud to show us evidence of his heroism. Then the people all got back into the canal, all talking about "the lampeel."

All the time my mother watched the young people playing in the flooded water at the canal, I could sense her concern for them, as well as her disapproval.

As we walked back home, I was pouting, still dejectedly wondering why we could never go swimming as I saw people do in comic books or in movies. I loved Esther Williams' films. She looked so graceful and happy in the water. Finally I said it to my mother: "Why don't they have any swimming pools for colored people?"

Every summer I saw lucky white children walking past our house each day in their swimsuits and carrying large bath towels on their way to the public swimming pools. I remember the irony of seeing them getting so tanned they looked almost colored themselves. At the pool near the Whitney Bank, an iron spiked fence let you see in, but we had to stay out. I saw that they had two pools—a safe wading type pool for tiny kids and a big pool for the more experienced. There was also a life-guard.

It hurt to see so many people reveling in pleasure and having it forbidden to you. It seemed everything that was fun was forbidden to us "colored people." My mother gave me many explanations and said many things to try to make me feel better, but I never could understand why things were the way they were, nor accept why they had to be that way.

Grandpa tried to do what he could about the situation after he bought a big truck. He would drive anyone who wanted to go for a two-hour drive to a place on the other side of the river called Lincoln Beach. This was the amusement park and beach set aside for the colored people of New Orleans. It was two hours away on the outskirts of town. Do you think that was fair? You think that was fair to a little kid?

Jo Anne makes her First Communion.

Cousin Jenny and the Infant of Prague

The French Quarter of New Orleans seethed with winos, tacky ladies, flaming smoky clubs, broken whiskey bottles, smelly cigar butts, and assorted lost souls. Yet deep within the Quarter existed worlds of contrast. These included the majestic St. Louis Cathedral, and behind it the piously placid Convent of St. Mary's Academy, with its caramel-colored nuns and, nearby, the home of someone known to us as Cousin Jenny.

It was my Aunt Shirley's Confirmation Day. Even though she was my aunt, my grandparents' youngest child, Shirley and her sister June were about my age and were the ones I grew up with in the house on Vallette Street. As was the custom in New Orleans, you visited everyone related to you, plus anyone else close to your family, to spread the wonderful news that you "made your Big Communion." This was a most special day in the life of a young Catholic. Besides being confirmed by an actual bishop, who invoked the Holy Spirit to witness this rite intended to proclaim strengthening of your faith against evils of the world, you got to choose a new name. It had to be the name of a saint you wished to emulate as a role model.

In a more worldly way, the day seemed even more special for a Catholic girl of eleven or twelve. Seeing herself in a pretty white dress, white veil, white shoes and stockings, she might envision her appearance as a bride not many years hence. A pretty white drawstring bag held her shiny new white or crystal rosary beads and prayer book (usually gifts from someone in the family, often a godmother or godfather).

A boy did not share quite as much in the material aspects of Confirmation. He wore a white suit because the nuns made him do it, but as soon as he got home he took it off.

Jenny was my cousin, even though she was much older than I. In fact, she was my grandmother's cousin's daughter, but everyone in New Orleans was a "cousin" even if he or she was not related to you. Jenny was strange, unlike any person we girls from Algiers had ever met. We called her "Jenny the Sage." How she acquired her home in the Quarter remains a secret, but it was spooky. Any footsteps nearing her house on St. Phillips Street would immediately set off two ferociously barking black dogs who kept vigil so that no one who had not been invited would dare enter. But we had gone there to show off Shirley. Not to do this would have been an affront, due to Cousin Jenny's esteemed position in the family. So, despite our great timidity, someone in the family rang the doorbell fastened to the tall gate of the high, unpainted fence in front of Jenny's house.

How she acquired her home in the Quarter remains a secret, but it was spooky.

After enduring a few minutes of vociferous barking, we heard barely, but definitely audible, a man's voice. As the high wooden gate opened slightly, we could see a benign-looking, light-skinned, round-faced man of medium height. It was Jenny's younger brother, Isaac, who lived with her and appeared able to control the dogs. Jumping up and down, they seemed at once happy to be with him and threatening towards us strangers. I, of course, was beyond terrified.

"Hello, Cousin Isaac," greeted the chorus from Algiers. Opening the gate wide enough for his visitors to enter, Isaac cried out, "Oh, wait till Jenny sees who's here!" Too involved with avoiding those dogs to note then the beautiful garden, I also failed to notice the sweet and lusciously growing fig trees around the house. These would have to wait for my attentions another time.

"Oh, just look at all the pretty ladies from over the river," said Isaac. "Now who is this? Is this June? Now who is the Confirmation girl? This can't be Shirley all grown up like that, but bless the Lord it is!"

We hesitated at the gate.

"Come in. Come on in!" he insisted.

"The dogs!" I pleaded mistrustfully. June spoke up, "That's Jo Anne. She's scared of dogs."

"Oh, they won't bite you," the man began, "not as long as they see me here. Come! Walk with me, little one," Isaac gestured. I clutched his big creamy hand with my tiny brown one. I had no choice now but to trust him. But it was impossible for me to trust those dogs. They were still barking and jumping as Isaac and I walked across the flower-lined path leading up the steps towards the door that met the long wooden porch along the length of the L-shaped house.

A sweet, praline-colored lady bounced from behind a dark green louvered door and threw her two hands up, clasped them and unclasped them, throwing them up again. Her eyes were almost unseen as her lids and the cheeks of her face met to smile a most pleasant welcome. Her hair was crinkly, soft silver-black, rolled and pinned into four separate twists on her head. And tiny simple gold hoops twinkled from her ears. She wore a high-necked cotton blue dress sprinkled with patterns of tiny white and black flowers. The dress covered her arms and went almost down to her ankles. But for all her modesty, she couldn't hide the fact that she had been amply endowed in the rear.

"Oh, praise be to God! Look who's here," Jenny exclaimed. "Isaac,

Isaac," she called as she walked, "Go put the dogs in the back!"

"This here is Margery's little girl. She's scared," Isaac explained. He seemed to understand that I would not feel safe until I was inside. "Here's your Cousin Jenny," he said to me, still holding on to my trembling hand. Cousin Jenny bent down to hug and kiss me a big smack. My eyes still on the dogs, I barely kissed the lady.

Isaac gently escorted me through the louvered door. "Now you can wait in here," he said. Then, he turned to usher the excited dogs off the porch, down the steps, and past another wooden gate adjacent to the side of the house.

I hadn't wanted to be impolite, but fear of dogs was something I could not yet logically handle. I waited safely inside the door as the rest of the group caught up with me. But my reaction of terror regarding dogs was something the family had come to expect and would have to consider and accommodate for a long time when taking me into new situations.

Cousin Jenny had warm hugs and kisses for everyone, especially Shirley. "Oh, look how beautiful and grownup you are. Oh my, June is getting so tall!"

I'd had time to notice that although the inside of the house was safe from the dogs, it seemed dark and slightly scary. Perhaps it was because the sitting room and the dining room were all one long and narrow room. Perhaps the tall mahogany furniture cast long shadows on a sunny Sunday. Maybe it was all those strange, old Victorian-looking pictures on the walls.

A big console radio was turned off. Table-sized statues of saints, lit candles, holy cards and photographed pictures of priests and nuns were on the mantel and everywhere else. Grandma Jenny at home in Algiers had a few of these things, but I'd never seen so many pictures and statues except in the convent where the nuns lived.

Isaac came from the kitchen with a frosty pitcher of lemonade and a tray of glasses. "Here's something to cool everyone off from the long trip." It seemed that once the dogs were quiet there was no sound except for the echoing voices the family reunion had wrought. Why was it still strange in this house? Ah, I thought I had it figured: There were no children here.

I continued looking around this oblong room while the older people fawned over Shirley's Confirmation dress, put money in her bag, and talked about this or that. I had already walked around with Shirley all morning, up and down Algiers, and had already seen how her Big Communion bag had been loaded with nickels, dimes and quarters from well-wishers.

Quietly, therefore, I examined the patterns in the delicately crocheted lace cloth that covered the round dining table. Then, I walked over to the pictures on one wall. Some looked so faded, but one of them I happily recognized as a priest at All Saints Church. "Oh, that's Father McKee," I exclaimed. "That's *our* priest. How did you get his picture?"

That question opened the door for a lecture on the Catholic Church by cousin Jenny. She knew Father McKee. She knew where he came from before he came to New Orleans, as well as the date and place he had been ordained. I was astounded, but the lecture had only begun.

Pointing to another picture, I said, "You know this priest too?" Cousin Jenny began the history of that priest, as well as that of his brother. They were the Albert brothers.

"I never knew two brothers in the same family could be priests," I said. Cousin Jenny proceeded to tell me the complete history of All Saints Parish.

"It was built by the Albert Brothers just in time for your mother to be born," she said, "and your mother Margery was the first baby to be baptized in that church in the year 1919."

After a bit, Cousin Jenny showed me a picture of a very pretty, colored nun. "This is my sister. Her name is Assise."

"Wow! You have a sister who was a nun," I said. "Is she dead?"

"No, she's not dead."

"Well, where is she? Does she live with you?"

"Oh, no," Jenny laughed. "She lives at the convent with the other nuns in the city."

I wondered what it must be like to have a nun as a sister, or a sister as a nun.

I was noticing how Cousin Jenny was different in a lot of ways. Usually when I asked adults questions, people told me that little children should be seen and not heard. But Cousin Jenny took time to listen and explain things. Maybe it was because she had answers. I also noticed that she had the same name as my grandmother. When I pointed that out to her, she said, "Your grandmother was named after me when she was born. We are both named Virginia Colla, but people call us both Jenny."

I noticed other things about Cousin Jenny, like the way her mouth drew up into some kind of poke after every few words, like someone without teeth. Up close, her eyes had a perpetual sparkle. It seemed she blinked only to hide them out of modesty.

By and by, Cousin Jenny saw me looking at a statue of the Infant Jesus of Prague with the little crown atop His head and the little smile. "You know, the Infant Jesus loves children," she said. "If you pray to the Infant Jesus, He'll bless you and give you what you want."

"Is that true?" I asked. "I prayed for something and I didn't get it."

"Well, maybe what you wanted, you didn't really need. You can't go wrong praying to the Infant Jesus. I know. He hears my prayers all the time. Sometimes He doesn't give you what you ask for, but He gives you what you need. Listen, I pray to the Infant Jesus every day. If He doesn't give me what I ask for, He lets me know why I didn't get it. For instance, I prayed to Him to wake me up in time for Mass. He always wakes me at 7:00 A.M. to go to 7:30 Mass down the street. One morning I woke up, looked at the clock, and saw it was 7:15. I said, 'Now what's the matter with the Infant Jesus, He didn't wake me up on time? I'm going to be late for Mass.' So here I am rushing and rushing and wondering why He woke me up so late this morning. So I get to church, it was 7:40 and Mass hadn't even started yet. For some reason, the priest didn't start Mass until 7:45. So you see, The Infant of Prague did get me up in time for Mass. He knew it was going to start late, so He let me sleep a little longer. Have faith in the Lord, Jo Anne. If He doesn't give you what you asked for, I'll bet He has a good reason."

She handed me a little booklet. "See this prayer to the Infant Jesus? Say it. He will always answer you. You go to Him in church and say this prayer. Tell me if He doesn't answer you."

Jo Anne opens the Dumas Dance Revue.

African Princess

One day the head nun at our grade school went on a rampage. It seemed some of the children in my class had been talking, and the exasperated third-grade teacher made all of us kneel down in the hall for penance. The principal grabbed the bigger boys four at a time and cracked them soundly across their backs with licks from the big stick that I can still hear. She then began to beat the girls the same way she had beat the boys.

When it was my turn, I stood up to face the nun. She looked at me and for some reason froze. She then dropped her arm holding the stick, turned and walked out of the building. I and everyone who had been kneeling behind me had been saved. I wondered what came over her, but I was more than relieved that I had not been touched.

Another time, my grandfather saw me at the dining room table writing, writing, writing. He asked me, "What are you doing there?"

"Writing lines," I told him.

"Well, how many lines?"

"We all have to write two thousand lines for homework," I said, "because them children didn't want to stop talkin' and Sister said the good have to suffer for the bad."

Grandpa scrutinized my paper tablet and saw that I had written about two hundred and seventy times, "I must learn how to obey."

"Uhn, uhn!" he said, "You are not going to write two thousand lines.

47

You have written enough."

"But, Grandpa, I have to turn in two thousand lines for homework tomorrow or I'll get in trouble!"

"Listen to me! You're not going to write any two thousand lines. That's too many lines for you to write. And you're not going to get into trouble. So don't worry about that. What's your teacher's name?"

"Sister Tekawitha."

"All right. When you go to school tomorrow, you hand in these lines and you tell Sister Tekawitha that I said this was enough for you to write and that I'll be there to talk to her at lunchtime. You go on to bed."

The next morning, everyone was all abuzz asking, "Did you do all them lines?"

They all knew I always did all of my homework. But nobody had actually written all of them. Some had reached five hundred, a few did seven hundred. One boy had stayed awake until midnight doing one thousand. Some had enlisted their older siblings' help and turned in the two thousand. Everybody was scared. We were only in fourth grade. Their eyes widened with astonishment when I admitted how few I had written. I told them my grandfather had stopped me. Then the bell rang. Though filled with apprehension, I told the teacher what Grandpa said, just as he'd told me to. And just as he'd promised, he showed up just before the lunch bell.

Through the classroom window I saw him walking up the front steps to wait in the hall. I can't tell you how immensely relieved I was to know he was there. I did not get into trouble. Certainly some classmates were envious that my grandfather had stood up for me. I had written the fewest number of lines in the entire class.

For some reason, it seemed my grandparents and my mother treated me as though I were special. I could never understand why. At the same time, I always felt somehow distant from everyone around me and somewhat removed from everyone I'd meet. Besides the most obvious aspect of being very different physically from my very fair-skinned mother, her subsequent remarriage left me the only person I knew bearing my last name: Green. Jo Anne Green.

I felt different—not better, not worse—just different. I felt somewhere within my mind that there existed some mystery regarding me that nobody would come right out and tell me. I was not allowed to act like everyone else. My upbringing was certainly very strict: I mustn't talk, walk, sit or lean this way or that. And if I happened to be with someone who showed the slightest inclination to expose me to even the most minimally wrong thing, I was gently but firmly removed from that person's presence.

When a boogie beat drew Barbara to dance the way the music moved her, I joined in the fun—which, I suppose, involved a little hip shaking on my part.

For example, one summer evening as a little girl at a church social, I was enjoying an ice cream cone with my good friend Barbara Jean while watching the records on the jukebox flip and play as people dropped coins in the slot. Everybody had begun calling Barbara Jean "The Queen" because of a role she had portrayed in a school play. When a boogie beat drew Barbara to dance the way the music moved her, I joined in the fun—which, I suppose, involved a little hip shaking on my part. I had noticed my grandfather standing not far away in the light by the front fence gate, but I thought nothing particular of it. At the music's end we stopped dancing and then I told Barbara I was going to run over by my grandfather to say hello, as I saw him beginning to walk over towards me anyhow.

Maybe I asked Grandpa for some money to play another song I liked on the jukebox. In any case, he gave me some money but leaned over and told me kindly, but firmly, "Now, Jo Anne, you did your part well, but don't you ever let me see you dancing again like I just saw you dancing with The Queen!"

I didn't know I had done anything wrong, but I couldn't offend my grandfather intentionally. I quickly went back to Barbara before she started up again. "I can't dance like that anymore," I said. "My grandfather doesn't like it." Yet, as I looked all about, I could see other young people dancing and jigging. So Barbara and I just stood and watched the records spin around and we talked about something else.

I wanted so badly to belong to something, to fit in. I wondered why I couldn't be like everyone else. What was behind all this?

Whenever I would ask about my own father, I was told that he had died. Later, when I'd think to ask how he had died, no one would tell me right away. Somebody once said he died in a car accident, but perhaps I fashioned this bit of detail to fill in one of the many informational census cards that would confront me perennially in grade school.

"Should I write in the name of my father that died or should I put down the name of the stepfather that my mother is married to now?" I'd ask the new teacher every year. Then I'd try to erase the complicated problem from my mind.

One day, my young aunts went sing-songing through the house to tease me with words that both shocked and stung. "Jo Anne's daddy was a African! Jo Anne's daddy was a African!" Scenes from Tarzan movies at first seared my little brain, but then they vanished because I knew this had to be just another mean joke my silly aunts were playing on me. How could my father have been African with a name like Green? Still I ran to my mother for comfort, consolation and negation of what my young aunts had said.

"Mama, they said my daddy is an African!" I cried.

Mama put her arms around me, looked me tenderly in the eyes, and told me, "Jo Anne, yes, your father was African. He was an African prince." This revelation was traumatic, to say the least, but my mother handled it gently. I could see by the look on her face that this was no joke and wondered why she'd never told me before.

"Your daddy's name was Kiptas Latimer Green," she told me. But despite the serious look on her face, I needed some proof, something tangible, to convince me that I really was the daughter of an African prince.

I asked my mother where she had met my father. She told me they met when he was studying opera at Xavier University in New Orleans. This sounded too fantastic to be true, yet it could explain why I'd always been so irresistibly drawn to music. I looked at my dark brown arms and my mother's very light face. This could explain why my skin, my hair, my nose were different from hers, although I clearly had her eyes. Again I thought of those horror images from Tarzan movies.

"Did he look like me?" I asked.

"I'll show you," she said gently. She reached into her bureau for something she must have been saving until she thought me old enough to appreciate it. I was now eleven years old. I already had seen one opera. Mama unfolded a picture revealing a very dignified man in a black tuxedo standing with the seven other men who comprised the Xavier College Male Octet.

"This is your father, Jo Anne," she told me. I could see he looked exactly like me. She told me my father was a very talented tenor who sang in Xavier University's opera productions. She added that he'd studied voice with a highly respected nun by the name of Sister Elise.

I could read the article under the photograph in the newspaper. Mama let me take time to absorb it. The male octet had been featured on the radio, and the program that had been sung was listed. It included the *"Ave Verum"* and other numbers that in time would become profoundly dear to my heart.

This was a most special moment for me. I felt unique in a way I cannot describe, just knowing who my father really was. His name was listed beneath his picture in the paper. The thought that he'd actually sung opera was wonderful to me, because I loved to sing. Oh, I loved to sing! I was not odd for being so attached to music; my father had loved it too. My mother gave me the article to keep for myself.

The totality of this revelation was a bit too much to comprehend all at once. My father did not look at all like the pictures I had seen of Africans. And except for his high cheekbones and the distinguished way he held himself, he appeared no more African to me than any of the other black men in the photo. But the news article said nothing about his being a prince, despite the fact that he did project a regal bearing. I asked my mother again, "Are you sure he was a prince?"

"If you don't believe me, ask Cousin Jenny," she said.

That statement was enough proof for me. Cousin Jenny was the expert on everything, a saintly and respected family historian, the sage of the entire Lombard/Colla family. Everyone knew Jenny never lied about anything. I believed my mother, but I was astonished that Cousin Jenny had awareness of this situation.

"You mean Cousin Jenny knows about all this too?" I asked.

"Yes, she does."

"Do Grandma and Grandpa know about this too?"

"Yes, they know."

"Well, how come nobody never said nothing about it before?"

"Because you were too little to understand."

After a very long, thoughtful pause, I asked, "Mama, does this mean I'm a princess?"

"Yes, it does. You are a princess, Jo Anne."

This was too much for my little mind to grasp. I suppose I was in shock. A few minutes before I had been Jo Anne Green, a bit of a misfit. Now I had discovered that I was Jo Anne Green, a princess. I needed some time to think about all this.

The next day in school, I needed to test my newly acquired identity on somebody for a reaction. I told my cousin Rudy, who sat next to me in class. Rudy was my close buddy; he was very smart and we shared a lot. I told him that my mother said my daddy was an African prince. I didn't know how he'd react, but I certainly did not expect him to do what he did. He got so excited that he ran up to tell the teacher.

But in his excitement Rudy confused the information and told the teacher I was a prince. "Don't be so ridiculous, Rudolph!" the teacher trumpeted to the entire class. "How could Jo Anne be a prince?" I was so embarrassed that I didn't dare attempt to explain. Completely mortified, I wanted the floor to swallow me up, and I never mentioned my true identity to anybody again for many years.

Jo Anne sings at college talent show.

Adventures with the Nuns

For whatever reason, it seems the Holy Family nuns took a liking to me as soon as I entered All Saints School near our home in the Algiers section of New Orleans. Back in those days, the sisters were not permitted to venture beyond the distance of a city block without a companion—female, of course. So with my mother's permission I was often chosen to accompany different nuns wherever they had to go.

I enjoyed these opportunities because they expanded my world by exposing me to people, places and situations I probably never would have experienced otherwise. This allowed me to observe a unique respect that ordinary citizens, black and white, accorded the nuns. And my unique access to convent interiors opened up the private world of women religious. I got to see them when they were relaxed and not just mysterious holy persons with stiff, starched, public personalities.

Perhaps back then the sisters felt I might become one of them, and for this reason exposed so much of their living to me. Indeed, later in my life, many of my best friends would be nuns and former nuns. One thing is sure: I was asked many times in my life if I thought I'd like to be a nun. The prayer, spiritual and charitable aspects of the life were certainly appealing to me, but the sacrifice of personal choices most certainly was not!

My gradual awareness of my own deep—though not overtly evident—independent streak made me cognizant of the definite problems I would have had with the total obedience factor of the religious life. So much of life was being denied to me back then; so much of my will deferred to that of others. I realized that if I were ever offered freedom or adventure I'd seize it in a heartbeat.

> *One time, I noticed in one bedroom a straightening comb, which was quite a surprise to me.*

Knowing this much about myself, then, I experienced the luxury of some personal selection: Sisterhood was but one option available to me; despite strict limitation of life opportunities for black girls and women back then, I felt somehow there would be other choices accessible to me in my time. But heiress Saint Katherine Drexel's generous purchase of a convent for the Holy Family nuns became a special cultivation ground for me. As a young girl, I was trained by the nuns to care for that legacy. I watered the lawn and scrubbed the front porch. I mopped, swept and dusted every single room in that edifice. Each bedroom had twin beds, except for the room of the Mother Superior, which had only one.

One time, I noticed in one bedroom a straightening comb, which was quite a surprise to me. I didn't know nuns still straightened their hair after making their vows! Of course, I asked Mama about it, and she replied that it was probably to help their hair lie more comfortably within the bonnet of the habit.

I cleaned the toilets and remember shock when the supervising sister instructed me that I had to use the rag and put my hand "down in the toilet" to clean it right. I dusted, washed and dried all the slats of all the Venetian blinds in that convent, and it seemed like there were so many I would never complete the job. The nuns got a little wooden ladder for me to climb so I could reach all the way to the very top slat. For this reason I was reluctant to have Venetian blinds in my own home for many years!

I washed all the baseboards in the hall, in the chapel, and in all the bedrooms. I polished the big mahogany piano in the living room, from its oblong lace-covered top to the eighty-eight black and white keys, to the three gleaming brass pedals at the bottom. Of course, I'd gently removed the scarf and replaced it afterwards. I rather enjoyed the polishing though. It made everything so pretty and shiny—especially the wooden prayer kneelers in the chapel. And one day the nuns removed all the chairs and kneelers to teach me how to wax and use the electric buffer to keep the high gloss on the beautiful hardwood floors.

I especially liked cleaning the chapel. From the small altar, the golden tabernacle covered with white cloth seemed to be watching me in a way I cannot explain. It seemed to be waiting, waiting for me to do or say something. Perhaps I anticipated being spoken to. Yet I felt fear in there all alone. I knew I was in a holy place and felt unworthy to be there. How I wished I could be holy! Sometimes I'd offer a little silent prayer as I worked and took care to genuflect in respect whenever crossing in front of the Blessed Sacrament. And I'd always bless myself with holy water from one of the tiny metal fonts on either side of the door whenever I entered or left.

The nuns had designated hours of prayer in chapel early in the morning and in the evening. On special days, each took turns praying alone in there for an hour around the clock. They told me that on certain days a priest would come and offer Mass for them and on other days he'd come to hear their confessions. I remember thinking how neat and convenient it must be to have Mass said right in your own house without having to walk for blocks to get there—especially if it rained.

I did wonder, however, what a nun could possibly have to tell in confession. I'd thought early on that just being a nun would have made you holy. Then one day I overheard a disagreement in the convent hall. A nun was asking the Mother Superior permission to borrow some of her nice gift paper to wrap a present for someone. The Mother Superior gave her a loud flat "No! It's too expensive. I paid good money for that!" This exchange stung my little ears! I had been taught that charity was one of the first laws of God and that selfishness was a violation of that law. I was stunned to hear someone who taught me these precepts was not practicing them herself! Now, I would not have been shocked at this type of selfishness from ordinary people, but I held nuns to a higher standard. Maybe this exchange was not sinful and perhaps there was more to it than I heard at that very moment, but I never expected a nun to not share readily with her sisters.

I dusted and polished the dining room and noticed how nicely and neatly all the china, drinking glasses, silverware and cloth napkins were set up on the beautiful dark wood table all the time for meals. I know it must have been one of the sister's duty to keep it looking this way, and in time this duty was transferred to me. Yet in comparison to my lifestyle at that time, this all seemed a bit luxurious for someone who had taken a vow of poverty. I was never however allowed in this room while the nuns were dining, although I could hear them sometimes enjoying pleasant conversation accompanied by dainty clinking of the chinaware. Sometimes I was given something to eat in the kitchen, which was itself very nice. Judging from what I was given to eat, the sisters were indeed rather good cooks.

One Saturday the younger nuns played a joke on me when I was helping them get ready to cook okra gumbo. Since they knew I did not like to make mistakes, especially with them, they kept giving me conflicting instructions. I was standing by the kitchen sink counter when one sister told me to wash the okra and wipe the shrimp with the cloth she'd handed me. This I did, although it did not seem to me to make much sense. About five minute later, another nun came by and told me, "Oh! No! You're supposed to wipe the okra and wash the shrimp!" She walked off, and I then followed the new directions. Soon an old, old sister came by shaking her head almost expressionlessly and said, "Somebody told you all wrong. Peel the shrimp first; then wash it. Then rinse the okra and wipe it." I suppose I should have been angry, but I didn't know anything about cooking at the time and they were just having some fun at my expense.

In the laundry room, which was detached and behind the convent, I washed the sisters' clothes. I starched some as I had been trained and hung them all up to dry on the line in the backyard. It was a mystery to me how they could manage wearing so many layers of garments, especially as hot as it gets in New Orleans.

One Saturday my best friend Jeanne came to help me with the laundry. We started a game, guessing whom the clothing belonged to. There was this one huge pair of stiff white underpants, much larger than all the rest. My friend said, "That must belong to Sister So-and-So because you know she's got a big, big butt!" We giggled softly for a few minutes as we continued the rest of the clothes on the line. Then one of us brought up the idea that maybe we would have to tell about giggling at the nun in confession. We had such strict consciences.

The sisters took me along when they went shopping to buy a gift for someone or to get groceries. I could help carry the lighter things. We didn't have to walk far, because bus drivers in New Orleans always let Catholic nuns ride free. One of the sisters would give me necessary coins for my own fare, but sometimes drivers would just let me on free because they knew I was with her. This was just one of many courtesies extended to religious of the Catholic faith in an overwhelmingly Catholic city.

One day a sister took me with her for errands across the river in New Orleans proper. Vendors were always near the Canal Ferry entrance, and on the way back Sister wanted to buy some peanuts for herself and a bag of potato chips for me. She asked the Italian vendor the cost, but he put one hand inside a moneybag that extended like an apron around his waist and with the other hand waved kindly and smiled, "That's all right, Sister." I couldn't believe my eyes or my ears. Sister thanked the man and away we went with free goodies. I thought, "I'll bet he was raised the same way I was raised, that whatever you do for the religious on earth, God notices in heaven. New Orleanians rarely charged a religious full price for anything, because it was generally felt that priests, sisters and brothers had given up a lot, were working for God, and were underpaid if they were paid at all.

Out of gratitude for the nuns at All Saints, every Christmas that I can remember, my Grandfather Manuel collected money from around the city to ensure they had a nice gift from the community. I know because, as penniless as I was, he collected money from me! Where did I get the dollar I gave him? I couldn't tell you, but Grandpa told me that for all the sisters gave to me I should consider it a privilege to contribute to them. Sometimes Grandpa bought them a turkey for Thanksgiving as well. He was always collecting and giving to All Saints Church.

I rarely knew where the sisters were taking me when they phoned for me. Sometimes I felt they just wanted me around. Yet wherever we went I would most certainly see something I'd not seen before. On one such occasion across the river they took me to the place they bought their garb: black stockings, black shoes, black shawls, black umbrellas. This was called the Nuns Supply House. Nearly anything you might want to buy for a nun at Christmastime would have to be black. Some communities of nuns did use brown. In any case, this was where you could buy these things.

One place the nuns took me might have totally blown your mind if you were not Catholic, but it was a feast for the eyes and I loved going there. It was called the Catholic Book Store and was near the French Quarter on a little side street. Why it was called a bookstore I don't know, as they sold a lot more than books. They carried a multitude of beautiful things that Catholics revere, love and use in their faith.

A profusion of rosary beads in every hue imaginable drew the eye. There were simple black ones and some much more ornate in crystal. These beads were not intended as decoration for someone's throat but were meant to be used. Did you know that the beads of a rosary and some of the spaces in between each represent a prayer? Saying a rosary sends up sixty-seven prayers. No wonder the rosary seems so effective in gaining heavenly favors.

You would not believe the variety of crosses and crucifixes also available at the Catholic Book Store in widely differing sizes and materials. Countless medals bore likenesses of Jesus, St. Joseph, St. Anne, St. Anthony, St. Theresa, St. Jude, St. Christopher, the Blessed Mother, and the Holy Spirit in the form of a dove. Mary actually had a category all her own that included Miraculous Medals and those of Our Lady of Lourdes, Our Lady of Guadalupe, Our Lady of Fatima, Our Lady of Prompt Succor, and several other designations. Naturally the store offered statues and statuettes. Popular were those of Jesus, of Mary, and of St. Joseph, as well as statues of Jesus, Mary and Joseph together: the Holy Family. Also included were statues of angels, St. Anne, St. Theresa, St. Lucy, St. Jude, St. Anthony, and—though he had not yet been formally canonized at that time—the black St. Martin de Porres.

Here were myriad candles in various sizes, widths and lengths. There were even vigil lights like the ones they had in church, in either the small or the large red glass holders. The store did sell religious books, including Bibles, catechisms, assorted prayer books, and scholarly books with titles I could not yet understand. I was drawn to reading tiny books with pictures on the lives of the saints. The nuns bought me one and then Mama went back and bought me others in the collection. How I loved those books! The nuns also bought me a little statue of the Infant Jesus of Prague, which I still have and cherish today.

All manner of sacred pictures and paintings adorned the walls. Counter bins held little brown scapulars, holy water fonts, holy water bottles, and other things too countless to list here. Yet each thing I've mentioned here held a spiritual meaning and was not a display of superstition or magic as some of our Protestant brethren charged. Catholics just believed that spiritual people gave spiritual gifts to remind others of their faith in God and of God's love. New Orleans was unique in its predominance of Catholics and Catholic culture, and the Catholic Book Store merely reflected that reality back then.

More Nunsense

My mother had taught me about New Orleans' unique, interesting past one summer when I'd expressed complete boredom about the city of my birth. She had gotten me a book, *New Orleans: America's Most Interesting City*, and after we read it together she had taken me for a walking tour of the *Cabildo*, the Cathedral, the French Market, and other legendary places within the city.

For many Sundays thereafter, Mama and I would walk around historic New Orleans streets. We'd stroll in and out of antique shops, and she'd point out sites as we went along. Mama always seemed to know so much more than anyone else about almost everything. We saw many pretty things, and I always felt bad that we could not afford to buy any of them. We just looked, talked and strolled. She was determined to make me realize, as she would say over and over, "Jo Anne, you live in the most interesting city in the United States!" Mama caused me to fall in love with an entire city.

The first time I visited the Holy Family Convent Mother House at St. Mary's Academy in the French Quarter, I was awed by its exquisite palatial beauty and profound history. As the huge door chime rang, I looked over my right shoulder and saw the steeple and the back view of St. Louis Cathedral. Waiting with the nun who brought me, I wondered if the pirate Jean La Fitte might have passed right where I was standing on his way to Pirates Alley.

I knew the Mother House was where my Aunts Sylvia and Aline had gone to high school. I recognized it from its picture in their yearbooks. I had also heard my mother say time and again that originally this building had been the Quadroon Ballroom, where in olden days white gentlemen would come to select a lady of color as a mistress. I thought this mere idle gossip until years later when I was doing research for a college history project and stumbled on to a little known section of the public library housing historic documents on miscegenation in New Orleans.

It was as if my mother had given dictation to the authors of those books some time before she was born! All she'd told me about the Quadroon Ballroom and more was written and recorded: Wealthy white gentlemen would come to the Quadroon Ballroom, sometimes while their wives were just down the street at the opera house, and choose women of color with whom they would set up housekeeping in a section of Rampart Street. Their wives they would keep in another part of town.

Right where I stood with Sister ringing the doorbell was where some of this notorious history took place. And now it was a nunnery.

A slightly stooped-over nun opened the huge door, and the two nuns embraced, alternating their white "horse blinder" bonnets over each shoulder. We were cheerily ushered inside. I sat alone in a beautiful waiting area in front of the awesome great hall while the nuns went to get the sister we had come to visit. I watched them vanish up a winding stairway that surpassed the one in *Gone with the Wind*. Then I let my eyes devour the other mystically beautiful things nearby.

A tiny chapel on my left held oodles and oodles of lit candles brimming over with cascades of dripped hot wax. The most gorgeous chandelier that I have ever seen hung from the ceiling in the middle the infamous ballroom. The floor itself was an exquisite work of art in high quality wood. The walls near me held ornately framed pictures of the Blessed Mother and one of the order's beautiful saintly foundress, Henriette Delille. There was a picture of Pope Pius XII, who was alive then, and the ubiquitous image of the current Archbishop of New Orleans, Joseph Francis Rummel.

That's when I learned that the nuns cared for many orphans, very poor girls that nobody wanted.

After I had breathed all of this in, the nuns returned and I was shown the quaint chapel upstairs and living quarters of students in residence there. That's when I learned that the nuns cared for many orphans, very poor girls that nobody wanted. These children were given life's basics, as well as a regular, and quite good, private-school education.

While the sisters visited some more, I was taken down the back stairs to wait in a serene, landscaped courtyard. Grass and garden were well tended, and there was a walkway that seemed to travel in an intricate circle. I learned later that it might have been a labyrinth, modeled on those in churches in France.

A young novice in white walked up and down the pavement reading prayers in solitude. Watching her praying so peacefully, I did ponder what it might be like to become a nun.

Not too many weeks later, they let me see firsthand.

Once more I was brought to the French Quarter for a ritual that was not performed very often. Several young black women were taking the veil. Their parents and selected friends had come to share this wondrous affair. It surprised me to see postulants march in white wedding gowns and veils, just like regular brides. The girls were given wedding rings and took vows, just like regular brides. Their vows, however, were of poverty, chastity and obedience. Everything was like a formal wedding, except for the lack of a physical groom. These women were to be brides of Christ.

They would give up the things of the world, and thus they were given new names for their new lives. After marching to a side room out of sight, their hair was shorn a bit by older nuns to effect the physical change of identities, and then the novices emerged in their new habits, but with white veils instead of the black ones the older sisters wore. The novices were presented individually by their new names to the gathering of witnesses. Amidst applause, some parents wept. I knew not if it was for joy or because of the loss of their daughters.

The sister who had brought me could hardly wait until we were on the trolley heading home before asking. "Jo Anne, do you think you might want to become a nun some day?"

I told her I needed time to think. I was just a little girl, not even in my teens yet.

While I was still in grammar school, I took dance lessons. One year, the nuns actually talked me into teaching the entire school how to tap dance. No, I'm not joking. In the evenings after school and sometimes during the school day, they had me take the students grade by grade and teach them a tap dance routine until they got it right. The nuns wanted to put on a big talent show with the entire school involved. Each of the nuns learned the dance steps along with the students so they could practice with them when I couldn't be there.

I didn't mind teaching all the children to dance, but what I minded very much was allowing the nuns to have someone copy almost all of my dance costumes, which had been originals designed for me alone by my dance teacher. Now there would be about twenty copies of my striking blue and black striped "Ball and the Jack" costume all over this small community of Algiers. There would be duplicates of my "Old Soft Shoe" outfit and of my ballet costumes—all of them cheap looking imitations.

There was never anything that the nuns asked of me that my mother did not make me do. But the uniqueness of each of these costume designs was something I felt belonged to me and to me alone. I had worked for them while other kids either played, watched television, or slept in. I had worked for them despite those who had ridiculed me for wasting time and money for "frivolities." While others slept warm in their beds, I had crossed the freezing river in the icy winters year after year to discipline myself for the rigorous demands of the dance for one special night of performance in June in a costume conceived just for me. I felt I'd earned the right to have something special that was my own and mine alone. I felt violated, truly violated.

I balked at allowing this until, I swear, one night in a dream the Blessed Mother appeared and told me she was pleased with the help I was giving the sisters with the dancing lessons and their talent show. I told Mama about the dream, and from then on I never complained. The show, a whopping success, earned the nuns lots of money for the school.

One time a nun I really liked named Sister Catherine brought us to the zoo. It had been many years since I had been to Audubon Park. Yet I still remembered where the peacocks were and the camels, the hippos and the monkeys. When we got to the cage of the monkeys, Henry Bellaire, who was always a cut-up, started feeding peanuts to the monkeys. One monkey was a bit more aggressive than the others and began grabbing all the peanuts Henry was flipping toward the cage. But Henry felt sorry for a little timid monkey who couldn't catch any. So he pointed his finger at the aggressive monkey and in his loud voice yelled, "Hey, you! You can't have anymore until you let your li'l brother catch some." The aggressive monkey put out his hand to beg from Henry. "No! I told you go get on the side," Henry yelled.

The aggressive monkey stared at Henry as if understanding every word he was saying. Henry yelled, "That's right! I'm talking to you. Get on away from here and let your li'l brother get some peanuts. You not gettin' no more!" So the aggressive monkey stared at Henry one more time and gave up and went towards the back of the cage to drink water. Henry proceeded to feed the smaller monkeys some peanuts, exuding pride in the fact that he had gotten control over the feeding situation. All of a sudden, however, the monkey who had been drinking water came bounding over towards the front of the cage and deliberately spat all of the water we thought he had been drinking into Henry Bellaire's face. Then the monkey jumped up and down, reveling in his revenge as if to say, "Ha, ha, ha. You thought you had me but I sure got you!" Henry's hair, face and shirt were drenched. This was perhaps the funniest thing any of us had ever seen, and we all cracked up.

Then the zoo attendant, a middle-aged man, came over and started fussing at Henry for feeding the animals. We were all astounded when Sister Catherine engaged the man: "Look! I see white children feeding the animals all up and down the zoo, but I don't see you telling them anything!"

The man answered, "White nor colored, it don't make no difference, S'ter. They not supposed to be feeding these animals."

Sister countered, "Well, when I see you go back there and tell that to some of them white children, then I'll tell this boy something."

The man walked away muttering something like, "When I see white children disobeying signs, I tell them too. White nor colored, don't make a difference. White nor colored, don't make a difference." His voiced trailed behind him.

Actually, I thought Henry was wrong for feeding the animals because an obvious sign forbade it. But Sister thought there was more involved. To be sure, there had been white children as well as adults disregarding the signs and feeding the animals. I had seen that for sure. So Sister thought the man was just picking on Henry and wanted to defend him. When the man backed down, she came over and asked us, "Y'all think I told him good enough?" I can't recall our response. I was just sorry the entire incident happened.

Sometimes people liked to call up and play jokes on me. One night when I was still in eighth grade, somebody called and took advantage of the fact that I could not place the voice. "Hello, Jo Anne, how you doin' darlin'?" the voice said.

I asked, "Who's this?" I thought it was one of those aggravating boys that I wouldn't have anything to do with down the street.

"Hi, darlin', can I take you to the picture show tonight?" the voice said.

"Who is this?"

"You don't know who this is?"

"No! Who is it?"

"If I tell you who it is, will you let me take you for a walk in the moonlight?"

"No, who is this?" Now the voice seemed strangely familiar. That's why I didn't just hang up.

"Oh, sweetheart, can't I take you to the picture show?"

The voice sounded like—but it couldn't be. "Sister? Is that you?" I said incredulously.

Then a roar of laughter almost tore the phone out of the wall. I could not believe my ears. "Sister Francis Paula?" I gasped.

It was my eighth-grade teacher, the principal of the school, playing a joke on me, Jo Anne Green. Sister asked to speak to my mother, but I couldn't get over how she'd played that trick on me. I didn't know nuns joked like that.

Let the Good Times Roll

During the early forties and fifties, there was not much for people of color to do for recreation in Algiers. One source of amusement was the Folly Theater on Opelousas Street. You climbed two flights of stairs outside the building to the balcony entrance. Inside, a white woman or man sold tickets and popcorn or candy from behind a windowed booth. "Dummy" was the name of the ticket taker by the inside stairs. I don't know what his real name was, but everyone referred to him as Dummy. Even if somebody said, "Hi, Dummy," on the street, he made guttural sounds and waved to acknowledge the greeting. No rancor intended, none taken. Yet, he frightened most people because he couldn't talk.

There was this aura of mystery about Dummy that none of us could ever hope to penetrate. He had intense eyes and hulking demeanor that communicated that he was not someone you wanted to mess with. With him in charge of the colored balcony, you could bet there would be no foolishness. Sometimes when the white ticket seller was not there late at night, or for whatever reason Dummy was alone, he would get behind the window and sell you a ticket. You didn't have to say whether it was for a child or adult fare. Dummy knew. He communicated with his hands and with his eyes.

If you came somewhat late and had missed part of the last show, sometimes Dummy would just let you in free. He'd just wave his hands, point towards the seats, nod his head, and you knew what he meant. If anyone did act up, get noisy, or bother someone, Dummy would shine his flashlight through the darkness precisely on the offender. Usually that embarrassment was sufficient to stop the monkeyshines. If Dummy didn't think you were repentant enough, he'd beckon with his index finger for you to get up and come to him. No one would dare to disobey Dummy, because they were afraid of what he might do.

Yet Dummy was a curiosity unto himself. Despite being scared of him, I often wondered if he was lonely all by himself, not being able to talk. I'd notice him standing alone off to the side wall, watching part of the last film of the night when no one was any longer apt to be buying a ticket. He seemed interested in the movie like everyone else.

At school we would talk about Dummy amongst ourselves. We wondered what happened to make him unable to talk, because he seemed to be quite intelligent. He was a strong-looking, well-built man. When he occasionally smiled at a young child, he was even handsome. People said that Dummy did not have a tongue. Children repeated hearsay that Dummy used to have a tongue but some white men had cut it out of his mouth to keep him from telling something he knew. That scared the bewillikers out of us. But no one could talk about the Folly without mentioning Dummy.

The Folly was the focal point of Algiers—the only place that everyone could and would go—colored or white, old or young, male or female. Everyone went to the Folly. It cost fourteen cents for a child's admission and a quarter for an adult. Though segregated, with colored patrons seated on the top balcony and whites on the floor level, the movie house was important to those of us who were black. The one other Algiers theater simply did not admit us. Besides being the only public outlet of entertainment colored patrons could frequent in

Algiers, the Folly was a vital source of information. We saw Lena Horne and Nat King Cole, as well as Jennifer Jones and Clark Gable, in the movies, and there were important newsreels allowing us to see Haile Selassie and Jessie Owens, as well as the King of England.

When the Folly took the risk of presenting films with racial themes like *Pinkie, Lost Boundaries,* and *Intruders in the Dust,* unbelievably long lines extended from both the white and the black entrances and almost wound around the block. But they did so without incident. These films made people aware of other lifestyles and what was happening in other parts of the world.

> *Sometimes I would look over at the white teenagers enjoying themselves at the pretty booths and tables and wonder why we couldn't sit down to eat our ice cream too.*

Besides, there was nothing else to do in Algiers. Back in the forties and early fifties, nobody had television.

June, Shirley and I would usually go to the Folly about twice a week, no matter what was playing if it was decent. The playbill changed about every two days. Occasionally some blockbuster came along that required a three or four day run. Sometimes friends of June and Shirley came along with us, and we'd walk the nine blocks to the theater together. Someone always had a pack of Wrigley's Gum, and we'd all share it—even if it meant someone would have to chew a half or even a fourth of a stick.

On the way home, June would invariably walk us towards Teche Street in the direction of the ice cream parlor to buy ice cream in a cardboard cup. We could not sit down in there, as it was a white establishment, but they would serve us inside. Sometimes I would look over at the white teenagers enjoying themselves at the pretty booths and tables and wonder why we couldn't sit down to eat our ice cream too. I knew we couldn't, but it made me feel bad. I hear we were fortunate. In some places in the South and even the North, we would not have been allowed to enter the ice cream shop at all.

June would share her ice cream with me if I didn't have enough money for any. She always had more money than the rest of us because of her work at the flower shop. As we walked along, we'd also pass the corner where the hot tamale man parked. June sometimes mixed the hot tamales in the box with the ice cream. We thought she was crazy, but one night we all tried it and it wasn't bad at all. Our little band strolled all over Algiers late at night, conducting our friends safely home. We three were always last to get home because we were together.

My mother always took me to see films with child stars like my favorite, Margaret O' Brien, and, of course, to the musicals. I had to see every single musical that came out of Hollywood. But I didn't really get to see them all. Mama avidly read the *Catholic Action* newspaper, and if the Legion of Decency gave a movie less than an A rating she would not let me go, no matter how much artistic merit the film might have or how much I cried, wheedled or pleaded. I remember that I had to wait until I was a grown woman before I saw one Betty Grable musical she would not let me see.

Westerns I would see with my grandfather. I knew how he loved horses, and I'd tell him when a "horse picture" was coming to the Folly. Each time, he would take me. He'd get dressed up, put on his after-shave lotion, and we'd happily walk along the Algiers streets together. I can't remember what we talked about, but I remember many people shouting a greeting to him. Sometimes I waited as people talked with him on the street for a few minutes. I got used to it. I knew Grandpa was well-liked and important. I would just be so proud that he was taking me to the movies. *Thunderhead* and *Black Beauty*, *Seabiscuit* and *Flicker*—I saw them all with my grandfather.

Many times within the dead of night, the telephone would ring. It would be someone imploring my grandfather to help them get their son out of jail. There was a certain distinguished legal man Grandpa would phone, no matter how late the hour, to learn if there might be a way to help the person out. Then Grandpa would wait up while the needed phone calls transpired. Usually something could be arranged for the son of the person who called.

There were not enough healthy social outlets for young people of Algiers once they'd graduated from elementary school, but no one did anything about it until my grandfather, Manuel P. Lombard, did.

From time to time, Grandpa would sponsor a dance at All Saints Hall to raise money for the church. He would hire bands such as Dave Bartholomew, with popular singers like Chubbie Newsome and Annie Laurie. He'd advertise the events on the side of his ice wagon. Since he was in charge, he always brought me to these affairs so I could watch the bands and listen to the famous ladies sing on stage. I would sit on a chair near the front door next to him. Afterwards he'd get some trustworthy person to walk me home before it was late. There was always a great turnout. People loved to dance and the money always went to the church.

Grandpa always had a hand in raising money for Carnival pageants for the church. One year he had me run for queen. I never thought I would win. I did not realize at the time how determined and indefatigable a worker my grandfather was. Perhaps there were people who thought very highly of my mother and me as well, but Grandpa raised over seven hundred dollars in contributions in my name for the church. Back then, that was a fortune. People said it was the highest any queen had ever brought in.

The pageant was wonderful. I wore a beautiful gown that my mother, my grandmother, and my Aunt Sylvia had made. I had a crown, a scepter and a mantel—all that shimmered and dazzled, and all were fashioned by my family. My cousin Rodney Lombard was king.

In addition to the pageant, people came dressed in marvelous costumes. A twenty-five dollar prize for the person wearing the best costume probably encouraged people to go all out in the masquerade department. And go out they did. There were gypsies, Indians, clowns, a toreador, old-fashioned girls, hoboes, and flappers.

Concessions included delicious hot dogs with chili, lemonade, soft drinks and popcorn balls. There was a great band, people dancing and having a wonderful time.

A latecomer to the ball stopped the show cold, just as Cinderella had. A man was dressed in my grandmother's blue dress and shoes, with her *tignon* wrapped around his head. He wore powder and lipstick and occasionally opened her purse, which he had slung on his arm, to freshen his make-up. Everyone had a great laugh at this hilarious sight. He was my Uncle Willie Lee, my Aunt Aline's first husband, who was always a lot of fun. He heightened the humor by dancing comically with the other men at the ball, which cracked everybody up. When the judges made their decision, Uncle Willie Lee won first prize.

Later during the night, while everyone slept, the sound of a broomstick falling on the back steps roused my grandparents, who were very light sleepers. In the morning, Grandma told us what had transpired. She said that after the broom fell, she could hear "tup, tup, tup, tup, tup, tup," the sound of footsteps running on the side of the house. She also heard "baramm" when somebody fell down. It seems a man mistakenly figured that money from the festivities might be in our house. Of course, the money had already been turned in to the rectory. But Grandma always kept her broom leaning just outside the back door, and when it fell it scared the prowler out of his wits and he ran. We could see the place in the mud where he had fallen down on the side of the house near the rose bushes. I bet they scratched him up good too. Those thorns could really hurt!

All Saints Church sponsored bingo on Friday nights. Adults frequented this weekly venture, as did a few school children—there were always good hot dogs and soft drinks sold. This was manned entirely by parishioners, but sometimes Father Walsh would come by and enjoy hanging around us, always with his cigarette fuming between his fingers. He was the worst chain smoker I'd ever seen.

The older priest in the parish, Father Albert, always had a joke to tell. One night he came by with his new companion, his dog Fleezie. He bought Fleezie a bottle of Coca Cola, bent over and held the Coke bottle in Fleezie's mouth. We watched the dog guzzle most of it down. Then, Father Albert stood up and drank the remainder of the Coke from the same bottle. Were we repulsed!

Sometimes priests seemed like grown-up kids to me. But we always loved them. The bingo games went on for several years, raising some good money for the church and basically being taken for granted. That was until Father Cassidy came from Mississippi.

Father Cassidy did not believe in dances or bingo. His arrival as pastor prompted an Algiers town meeting, with standing room only. People argued that dances and bingo assured support of the church, but Father Cassidy contended, "Make a five dollar contribution in your church envelopes on Sunday. That'll support the church." Algierians pleaded, but Father Cassidy would not budge, even after Grandpa met privately with him. This ended the era of Catholic Entertainment as we knew it in Algiers.

Grandpa figured that Father didn't understand how well-behaved and peace-loving the Algiers people were. He said, "Father is afraid somebody will come to a dance, get drunk, and start shooting. I told him we did not have trouble like that in Algiers."

Perhaps Father Cassidy did just want to avert a possible tragedy. Most probably he acted based on his experiences in Mississippi, which was quite different from New Orleans. But for most of us, it was just depressing.

Jo Anne on her wedding day.

Balls and Ballgames

Grandpa had decided after his sons came back from the war that he would create an outlet for some of the young people in Algiers. He started and coached a baseball team. They would be called "The Lombard Ice."

Like a bolt from bluest heaven, Algiers felt a new kind of excitement. Guys of all ages came around to our house to try out for the team. Pitching and catching, running and batting practice all transpired in our back yard. Suddenly there were baseballs, bats, mitts, gloves, bases, and other pieces of sporting equipment strewn about the back porch. One very exciting day marked the arrival of the red and white baseball uniforms. There was even a miniature one for my little brother Butch, who would be the team mascot. My cousin Rudy Lombard was the bat boy.

The ball games were first played in a relatively new playground near the levee, but for some reason this area was abandoned and the games then took place farther back in Algiers near Landry High School at what became the Fox Playground. Things progressed and the team began to attract a lot of attention. There were now hot dog and ice cream vendors, and one stellar night there was a big dedication graced with attendances by the mayor of New Orleans, De Lesseps "Chep" Morrison, and Morris Jeff, Sr., of the New Orleans Recreation Department. Now Grandpa was in an even better position to keep a lot of young people straight and a large segment of people entertained.

A lot began to change. All the talk now was baseball this and baseball that. Teams from the other side of the river would come to play the Lombard Ice. And the Lombard Ice ventured to the other side of the river to perform. Grandma Jenny would make sandwiches for the whole Lombard Ice Team. June, Shirley and I would form an assembly line in the kitchen to prepare food for the team. Grandpa, by this time, had a big new red truck and would drive all the guys to the games safely in the back. It seemed everybody began to affectionately refer to my grandfather as "Unk."

A short time later, Grandpa decided to coach a girls' softball team. They wore blue uniforms. Now Algiers had a baseball team and a softball team to keep its young black men and women occupied, focused, and out of trouble.

Meanwhile, Aline and her girlfriends began a Carnival club called "The Westside Revelers." They initiated dances and debutante balls to present young black ladies properly to society. There were club meetings and other socials. They all paid dues and raised enough money for a big ball around Mardi Gras. Engraved invitations were sent out and a band was hired. They had me tap dance and acrobat for additional entertainment. Because he was the only one everyone in Algiers trusted, Grandpa would be at the door to receive the admittance cards.

After the first year, however, a rift emerged in this club. As a result, some remained "The Original Westside Revelers," and Aline and most of her friends founded "The Girlfriends Club." For many years Grandpa continued to be at the door of the ball held by this second group, while I became the souvenir girl in costume who greeted everyone entering in their fine new ball gowns and tuxedos.

One year the ball theme was "The Red Shoes." June and Shirley enacted the story with another ballerina whose name I can't recall. June was the Lover; Shirley, the Shoemaker. Another year, the theme was "Marie La Veau." As the souvenir girl at the front door, I'd dressed as a witch doctor with a mask—grass skirt and all. When the dancers arrived and spied me in my outfit, they begged me to join them in their skit. My grandfather told me to go ahead, he could give out my souvenirs for me and accept the admittance cards while I helped the dancers. So, they took me to their dressing room and explained the dance plan. At a certain point in the routine, they wanted me to sneak out from behind palm trees, then gesture with my hands as though to put a spell on Marie La Veau. Then I would take a dramatic pose onstage as I watched her frenzied dance. Finally, I would dance around with them in a circle and follow them off the show floor.

This sounded like fun, so I joined in. They hadn't known at the time that I was a dancer too and also didn't know I was a ham. I didn't go too far, just enough to make the scene a bit more enjoyable for all than it might have been without me. The dancers complimented and thanked me, saying they didn't know I was going to be so good. Then I returned to my souvenir post by Grandpa and Aline brought me some delicious petite sandwiches and punch.

Some Algiers men started a Carnival club of their own called "The Jugs." They likewise held balls and parades through Algiers. They also did community things such as seeing that each black child in Algiers had a Christmas gift. My Uncle James belonged to this club. His good friend, Harrison Martin, who was largely built, dressed as Santa. This was the first time I'd ever seen a black Santa Claus. It was weird, even though I knew it was Mr. Martin.

Each year Aunt Aline would gather children at somebody's house and get refreshments together for a nice little party. Then Harrison

Martin would come in wearing his red and white suit, his fake beard, carrying a big sack and heaving his "ho, ho, ho's." The children really believed he was Santa Claus. I could tell by their faces. Mr. Martin really seemed to enjoy himself too. He was another person who genuinely liked kids and was nice to them every day, not just on Christmas.

How dare her Aunt Aline belittle her by expecting her to accept a dark-skinned doll?

One Christmas, Aunt Aline bought brown-skinned dolls for all her nieces. She was always trying to make people happy. One niece, who shall remain anonymous, hated her doll and threw it on the floor, insulted. How dare her Aunt Aline belittle her by expecting her to accept a dark-skinned doll? It took many years for this particular niece and many other people to develop a good self-image as black people. But that reaction, though shocking, can be understood when one examines the kinds of negative stereotyping that had been perpetuated for years. We blacks had been psychologically taught to hate our own images. Some of us did not buy into the sinful fallacy. Unfortunately, many of us did.

Color casting was a particular problem in New Orleans, with all its different shadings. People were treated certain ways based on their skin coloring and the grade of hair they were born with. Nothing good was expected of anyone of a dark skin caste, whether the person lived down to this expectation or not. Everything good was expected of a fair-skinned person, whether he or she chose to live up to this or not, or even had essential ability.

These negative stereotypes were innocently perpetuated by some of the beloved but misguided black nuns who taught us. I noticed that in the yearly Nativity play, the part of the Virgin Mary was always given to a girl with extremely light skin and straight hair (which was considered "good hair" in those days). Year after year I noticed this trend, but I never heard anybody say anything about it. The hair or the skin—I had neither of the desired criteria, so I had given up on ever getting that role, and I never did.

Long before reaching the age for graduation from All Saints elementary school, I had decided to attend Xavier Prep High School because I had seen the caliber of their musical program and had realized long ago that music was an essential part of my life. I had definitely decided on a musical career as soon as I saw Mario Lanza sing in the movie *The Great Caruso.* I have to admit that this was coupled with the knowledge that my father had sung in operas at Xavier University and that his vocal coach still taught there. Xavier Prep was a direct pipeline to the Xavier University Opera Department that I wanted to be a part of. That the nuns at Xavier Prep were all white never entered my mind. I'd had two aunts attend Xavier Prep, and that was enough for me.

The principal of All Saints, a black nun who in fact made all the decisions about who got which parts in the plays at the school, cornered me during seventh grade to ascertain my high school intentions. She became incensed when I told her I planned to attend Xavier Prep. I thought she'd be pleased, but she tore into me with the most racist comments I had ever heard to that date. "Why all y'all flock to the white sisters after we work with you for so many years?" I was just shocked. I thought brides of Christ were brides of Christ, nuns were nuns. That some were of different races did not matter to me, and I never dreamed it mattered to them either.

Sister was angry with me, but I didn't really care. Nothing could have dissuaded me from attending Xavier Prep.

The irony of the situation heightened three years later when as a sophomore at Xavier Prep I was studying Latin, which I loved. The sisters (who happened to be white) informed my class that we were going to do the Nativity story in Latin for the school at Christmas. The part of the Blessed Mother would have to be portrayed by someone of good character who was also very good in Latin, because the entire play had to be spoken in Latin. This was so important that the nuns were going to consider girls from all the Latin classes before making a decision. I thought for a second, "I'm pretty good in Latin." But as I took a sobering look around the classroom and saw all the girls who could have passed for white if they wanted to, I realized I didn't have a prayer. I put it out of my head. Within a few days, however, the announcement came that the person chosen to be Mary was me.

After I began high school, I couldn't give out souvenirs at the balls anymore. I had too much work to do and naturally became involved in my own school activities. But even long after I had gotten married, my grandfather was still in demand at the ballroom door.

Eventually, as my uncles married and had families to support, as the other young men of Algiers went to high school or college, as more options became available, the Lombard Ice, just like the Negro Leagues, ceased to exist. But the Girlfriends continued for many generations with their grand balls. *Et les bon temps roulait, roulait, roulait!*

A Park Forbidden

I need to set the record straight. There have existed persons of African descent who have been Catholic popes as well as canonized saints. Nevertheless, these persons were not expressly identified as *black* saints. They were taught about to me as saints—neither black nor white, just saints, period!

Perhaps some time before the settlement of the United States, urgent necessity for the specification of persons as simply black or white did not exist, for the distinct polarization of African-American people from white people did not have such purpose elsewhere as it did in the United States. In other words, outside of the United States, a person's race was not considered the most important thing to know about him or her. I had heard of this type of thinking and had read about it, but I perceived and understood this reality only when I did venture out of the United States. This enlightenment occurred when I visited my son studying in London. He took me also to Paris.

From that distance I could see with more clarity that there is indeed a stifling, even arrogant mindset unique to the United States that comfortably narrows thinking about people when it comes to race. I had also in time learned many things about Africans that had not been taught to me in the limited history lessons offered me in American Schools.

In Catholic high school I did learn of a St. Augustine, for example, who was a brilliant and most celebrated teacher, philosopher, theologian and doctor of the church. I was not taught that he was black, however. In Catholic school I did learn of his mother, St. Monica, who had prayed many years for him to turn from a sinful life before his great conversion and the development of his magnificent teachings. I was not taught that she was black.

Reading on my own, I did learn of a St. Benedict the Moor in a little book of saints. I was not sure what a Moor was, but I thought that the picture of him resembled a black man. So mystic and mysterious he looked. In time my curiosity would be satisfied.

I heard of St. Peter Claver, a strong advocate of the concerns of black people. I was gratified at his special interest, even though he was not black but a wonderful, loving Spaniard. I noted the special devotion that my grandfather and many other black men had towards him. Sometimes I would fantasize rituals that might be employed to revere a real black saint—if we only had one.

In the fifties, blacks in New Orleans were not allowed to use recreational establishments reserved for whites, nor were they permitted to rent white-designated establishments for business or any other purposes. One time, some of my elementary school mates were arrested for just playing in the playground next to All Saints School, because even though they rarely used it, this playground had been designated for whites only.

I suppose I should have been arrested too, because Father Walsh, a white priest, had told my class that we had the right to go in there and play at recess time. So we opened the gate, went in, and swung on the swings, slid on the slides, drank from the cool bubbly fountains, sat in the nice tree shade on the cool grass and watched boys toss a ball back and forth. Father Walsh stood nearby and watched us. It was a lovely spacious playground that nobody ever used. There were no white children left in the neighborhood, for they had all grown up and moved away, leaving it and their parents behind. The park was crying out for some children to use it. Yet for the previous eight educational years, my classmates and I had to play in the hot, hot New Orleans sun that bounced blindingly off the white of the narrow oyster-shelled street between the side view of the fenced off, forbidden playground and the side of the rectory. We did, that is, until Fr. Walsh finally gave us permission to "break in."

Sometimes I wondered why some white people were so nice while others seemed to hate the very sight of us. I wondered how Father Walsh could be white and stand up for us and how some Algiers residents could be white and hate him. But I'd known Father Walsh since I was in the third grade. He'd taught me catechism and heard my confessions. He'd prepared me for Confirmation, where he taught me about courage and faith.

It certainly took courage for my family and friends and I to remain black Catholics when many other blacks around us called us names and were mean to us because of our Catholicism. Even years later when my friend Dolores died, this meanness stood between a distant view of her coffin and my attempts to tell her goodbye. It had never mattered to Dolores that I was Catholic, and it had never mattered to me that she was Baptist. We were teachers, co-workers and friends.

Dolores and I had remained in touch even after our assignments sent us to work at separate schools. We'd shared confidences and a passion for good books. And we partied together when we could. She'd inspired me when she attained her master's degree despite her battle with ulcers. Her brother, then my co-worker, told me her ulcers had become cancerous. Before I could even visit her, she died.

That bitter night as I innocently tried to enter the Baptist church in uptown New Orleans where her remains lay, a group of black women swarmed towards me, "Get out of here, Catholic woman! We don't want you in our church!"

Startled, hurt, and in utter disbelief that people of my own race could be so heartless and cruel to me in an hour of grief, I pointed towards Dolores' coffin and stammered, "But I just want to say goodbye to my friend."

"Woman, we told you we don't want you here. Get out!"

I recognized Dolores' brother from behind and wanted to call him for assistance, but I did not want to add embarrassment to the grief I knew he and the family already bore. He was sitting way up front just next to Dolores. Tearfully, into the dark humid night I turned away, doubly grieved and traumatized as I realized I would never in this life get the chance to see my friend again.

It also took courage for us to remain Catholics with the disappointment and discomfort we felt as we learned that many white Catholics did not even want to sit next to us in church.

And yet it also took courage for us to remain Catholics with the disappointment and discomfort we felt as we learned that many white Catholics did not even want to sit next to us in church. It took everything we had for most of us to handle the dual isolations of being black and being Catholic. But Father Walsh had stood alone with us when it counted. He was white and different. He'd visited my grandfather's house, and I'd seen him visit my friends' homes. I'd often wonder how he, as well as the other white priests we'd had as pastors, could have given up an entire life to come and take care of our spiritual needs. We knew it took courage for Father Walsh to do what he did. We loved him, trusted him, and would have followed whatever he'd said.

I remember the first day I met him. It was lunchtime and I was in the third grade. For some reason, Father Walsh would come over and tease me and my best friend Jeanne Marie. We noticed he chain-smoked and his fingertips were stained yellowy-brown from constant cigarette use. Sometimes he seemed very tense and nervous as he tried not to smoke. I think now that the presence of my friend and I helped calm him down.

The hot sun had beat his incipiently balding forehead beet red. Every day he would come over, look at what we had for lunch, and create something disgusting to say it looked like. If we had spaghetti, he would say we were eating white worms. If we had hash, he'd say we were eating dog food. If we had rice he'd say, "Oh! Warm maggots today!" He'd tease us and nobody else the entire lunchtime. We'd laugh and plead, "Leave us alone, Father, so we can eat." But he'd get such a kick out of teasing us, and we always knew it was all in fun. But if we could gulp our food down before we saw him coming over, we would try.

There was a time when Jeanne Marie and I were about in seventh grade and he acted as sort of a protector. Jeanne and I were walking behind the rectory after eating lunch to get some shade on the other side of the oyster-shelled road. Some older boys and girls were standing near a tree next to the park. Fr. Walsh looked extremely upset as he stopped the two of us and said, "Don't go over there, Jo Anne. Don't go over there, Jeanne. Don't associate with trash. Stay over here. They don't care anything about their immortal souls!" When we looked across the street to see what he could be talking about, I recognized two of my male cousins, one older, one younger. There were some excited screams from the girls and I could see that they were all over there taking turns kissing on the lips in broad daylight. That was a definite, unqualified no-no in our house and our church at the time. They all knew better. I was truly disappointed in my cousins. I couldn't believe how they could stand there and do that right in front of Father.

Perhaps it was then and there that Father Walsh had figured that had they been allowed the use of normal children's outlets, such as the park for whites only, they might not be experimenting with adult things. But I knew he was concerned and upset. So Jeanne and I just stayed there and talked with him until the bell rang.

The only time Father Walsh did anything that Jeanne Marie and I might have thought questionable was really laughable in itself. You see, there were some years when the old school was being razed in order for the new brick school to be built. Father John Albert, the old pastor, was using money that an aunt left him in her will, to have the school constructed. During that year we had classes on the platoon system in the church. At lunchtime, Jeanne and I had the duty to sell candy on the church porch behind the rectory when Father Albert, always so ebullient, turned and waved to us as he was going up the back steps of the rectory. He reached up for the handle of the back door, but missed and fell backward down the steps flat onto his back and hit his head. Jeanne and I looked at each other in stark terror, because we both thought for sure that Father Albert, as old as he was, must have died.

We didn't know what to do. He was lying on the ground like a dead man. But just as we started to go over there, he got up and walked right straight up the steps and, not missing this time, opened the back door and went into the house. He must have just knocked the wind out of himself. We both heaved big sighs of relief. We guessed that he must be all right, but we were still both scared. We were trying to decide whether we should try to find Father Walsh, when suddenly he appeared inside the little gate near the shell-topped street. We were again relieved and glad to see him. Before we could say anything, however, he stopped and asked us, "Did Father Albert just fall down the back steps?"

"Yes, Father," we answered seriously in unison. Whereupon Father Walsh cracked up into loud laughter as if this were the funniest thing he'd heard in his entire life. He slapped his leg it was so good. Then, he walked up the back steps and went into the rectory to see about the pastor. Jeanne and I just looked at each other. We didn't know what to think. We would have thought it would be a sin to laugh at an old priest, and besides we would never have even thought to laugh because we were so scared he might have died. But after we saw Father Walsh laugh the way he did, we broke out and laughed at the whole thing to ease the tension.

Well, that was the only thing I ever saw Father Walsh do that might have been slightly wrong. And now, decades later when I think about it, it really was so funny that I can hardly stop laughing about it myself.

For all of two days we enjoyed recess time in the lush, lovely, green park next to our school that was supposed to be for whites only. But the nuns feared for our safety and told us after a couple of times not to go in there. White people would drive around the block, slow down and stare at us. They would call up their friends and neighbors to come stand on their porches and glare at us. A police car circled the block but did nothing. The neighbors requested that a white high school drive its football team to practice in the park for a while so the black people could not claim that the park was not being used by anyone. People even threatened to bomb the rectory. They called Father Walsh a traitor. The nuns feared for the priests' safety now as well as for ours and told us to stay out of the playground for a while.

By the time the whole thing blew over, I had graduated from elementary school and was on to high school. But I'll never forget the experience of "trespassing" on a forbidden park that should have been open to us in the first place.

Jo Anne records "Think of This" album.

A Light Will Rise

Within a few weeks, I graduated and put playgrounds and playtime behind me for Xavier Prep High School, where I would meet many new friends. And I met the Blessed Sacrament nuns, dedicated white women who served to prepare young black men and women like me to think, to go farther, to open closed doors and closed minds, to help change the world for the better in various ways, settings and times.

Most of us who went to Xavier Prep would attend and graduate from Xavier University. My friend Jeanne Marie would eventually earn a master's degree from Tulane University, which in an earlier time would not even allow black people to walk on the campus. My cousin Rudy Lombard would in time lead the resistance to racially segregated lunch counters in New Orleans. Despite death threats, he eventually won. He pursued and earned a doctorate. He wrote a book, owned several businesses, and ran a good, if unsuccessful, race for mayor of the city of New Orleans. I consider Henry Bellaire—he who cared enough to feed monkeys at the zoo–to be extended family, as he was always at our house. He worked for a time delivering ice for my grandfather. He attended St. Augustine, a private school for boys, and became a dean at Southern University of Baton Rouge, Louisiana. Harold Vincent, the quietest boy in our class, attained a doctorate in physics. He is now dean of the College of Arts and Sciences at Xavier University and is also a deacon of the Catholic Church.

As for myself, in high school I went on to win, among other things, an audition to sing an operatic aria, *"Printemps Qui Commence,"* with the New Orleans Philharmonic Symphony Orchestra. The event was broadcast on radio and my name and young age was publicized in the newspapers.

I did have a dream world, but of necessity I was extremely practical. First of all, I was realistic enough to know that in the South as it was then there would be no future for my high aspirations. Yes, I had performed with the symphony, but that was a stroke of luck, a blessing, because it was not televised and no one other than persons involved with the program knew I was black. But the door had opened for me, and like Cinderella's glass slipper, no one could take it away from me. Other blacks, noting this door ajar, proceeded to audition. It was feared that there were too many talented blacks who might in essence "take over." Thus an ordinance was promulgated forbidding the performance of blacks and whites on the same stage.

I was accustomed to such shenanigans, having grown up in the South. But you see, I'm one of those persons who knew how to cool it when necessary while obtaining my goals in silence. I was going to make it one way or the other, one place or another. My dancing teacher was always talking about New York City. Perhaps I'd find what I needed up north. I was creative and a good planner. I would obtain my Vocal Music Degree from Xavier and then go find my place in the world, while the South took its silly old time to grow up. I was resolute to get on with my own life on my own terms.

Adhering to my plans, I created a way to deflect suitors, because I wanted no reason to remain in this backwards atmosphere. I had no plans for marriage, so I seriously penned a list of ten nearly impossible standards for any suitor or a husband. Guys trying to date me were shown the list. Some laughed. Tough! I didn't date them. I'd created the list to deflect guys just like them. But if a man should come along who happened to fit the list, I'd consider him. Because of the problems my mother faced with her marriages, I was certain it was better to present criteria that were opposites of what I'd seen in my stepfathers.

Yes, dating might be nice, but I needed time for study, for practice, for assignments.

The fact that none of them had been Catholic did not go unnoticed by me. So I made devout Catholicism the first qualification for any beau of mine!

Other prerequisites demanded he be a musician or possess sufficient knowledge of music to understand its importance to me. He must be kind, unselfish, thoughtful, intelligent, a good provider, handsome, show indications of being a good father. He must not believe in divorce and must really love me. The list helped me save time and trouble, because the assets God gave me somehow attracted many guys, but most were time wasters. Yes, dating might be nice, but I needed time for study, for practice, for assignments.

Many people do not understand the demands of college. Most do not realize that the study of music courses is highly cerebral. I utilized every free moment I had for assignments. That meant I did homework on the buses and on the ferry ride across the river twice a day. In addition to our challenging music courses, we music majors took the other difficult courses that other students did—psychology, theology, physical science, European History, logic, English literature, biology. We further had to practice our instruments, do our coursework, and perform assigned portions of a Beethoven Sonata for a weekly grade. Plus, those majoring in voice had to work on vocalizations and art songs in foreign languages. We also had to memorize these pieces in addition to those taught in performance concert choirs, and we rehearsed until nearly midnight many weeks for the yearly grand operas. I think in all of college I only attended two dances, and I never had time for football games. That's how busy we were.

By second year, all the music students knew each other. The class with which I entered became like a family. We all hung together, always talking about some aspect of music. Some were not quite as advanced in several ways. For example, some had not been previously exposed to the language of music nor the names of composers. There was this one class we took three times a week with the symphony conductor, Mr. James Yestadt. He was very key to our personal expansion in music. Every Friday we each gave an oral presentation of a classical work we had chosen to listen to during the previous week. Ah, yes, this was our sight-singing and ear-training class. Well, as most composers had names that were not American, the mispronunciations of the French, German, Polish and especially Russian names were hilarious—even side-breakingly hilarious—to those of us who by grace knew better. More than one time the mispronunciations were too laughable for even the teacher to control his amusement. He'd apologize, of course. But Fridays were always a riot. We learned a lot, though, from this course and this instructor.

During second year, one of my classmates tried to date me. I brought out my list. After reading it, he telephoned me. "Jo Anne, okay, I admit I don't have the qualifications. I don't measure up to your standards, but I know someone who does, and you know him too!" I asked who that could possibly be. He taunted: "Somebody in our class." I said, "No, that's impossible."

He said, "No, it's true. He'd be perfect for you. He's a close friend of mine and I know him. He has every qualification on that list. His name is Melvin Tardy."

"Melvin Tardy? That cocky boy?" I said. "I can't stand him."

"That's just on the outside, Jo Anne. He really is a good person."

"But he's not *Catholic*."

"All right, no, he's not Catholic, but he's everything else on that list.

And nine out of ten is a good ratio and deserves a chance. I just know if the two of you ever got married you would produce all musical geniuses!"

Now, I really was not looking for a boyfriend. Yet next time in class, I quietly scrutinized Mel. I still saw things that irritated me, but I did try to see the qualities that his friend hailed. No matter, our determined friend played cupid between us so much that by year's end it was safe to say we were inseparable.

Mr. Yestadt played a part in this that he didn't know about. It must have been a Friday because we'd listened in class to the "Overture to Romeo and Juliet" by Tchaikovsky. The haunting music ran through my head all day. I needed to rush home and change because our Concert Choir had to sing that night, and I always loved a little white Juliet dress that Shirley had bought for me. So I wore it that night. After our performance Mel asked if he could bring me home. I told him I lived across the river in Algiers. (Most guys were afraid to come over there.) He said, "Okay!" So there we were, standing and waiting at the landing for the boat to come. The moon was full and it was so nice by the water. I was in my Juliet dress and that "Romeo and Juliet" music from earlier in the day kept running through my head. I thought to myself, "Could this be the one?" The boat came and Mel accompanied me home all the way without a car. I began to see some admirable qualities surface that I'd not seen before. Also, he was completely different with me than he was at school.

We didn't have money to date. But Mr. Yestadt gave us free tickets to symphony concerts. Mel and I attended these together. We began to sit next to each other every class, ate lunch together, rode the bus together, and walked down Canal Street holding hands while looking into store windows and dreaming together all the way to the ferry landing. Then one summer day, Mr. Yestadt took the choir to Notre Dame, Indiana, to sing. On the way, I'd say Mel and I were falling in love. But walking in the evenings by the campus lake, I'd say we were definitely in love. Little did I know what God was planning.

By junior year, I felt we could make it even though he was not Catholic. He had, after all, taken every theology course that I had taken. He knew what I needed to do in my religion. Besides, I found him head and shoulders more decent, respectful and moral than any Catholic boy I knew. By senior year, I decided that I would definitely marry Mel, even though he was not Catholic. But during that year, he totally surprised me. He had secretly been taking instructions and became a Catholic. Does God love me or what? Now I had ten out of ten on my list!

As it happened, I graduated earlier than Mel did. I accepted a job at Charity Hospital as a music therapist for the psychiatric wards. This was a very difficult job, but I had an encouraging supervisor who seemed very much in my corner. After a year I realized I made enough money to support us both. I had planned our wedding down to the penny even before I'd had a job.

Mama and I had fun going around Canal Street stores to find the perfect gown. Mama didn't have to pay for anything because I had been careful with my money. We ordered the flowers and the cake and saw to the dresses of the bridesmaids and took care of everything else. Nelson Francis, my life mentor and vocal instructor, offered to provide the music for me. I wondered how that would work, because most of the groomsmen were opera singers, as were the bride and groom.

The big day came and Grandpa gave me away. It was a beautiful ceremony. The choir performed my beloved *Ave Verum*. Nelson Francis sang the *Ave Maria* as I prayed and presented a bouquet to the Blessed Mother of Jesus. All of the music was beautiful. I had managed to plan a modest, simple, yet elegant and radiant wedding. A most beautiful aspect of it occurred as I turned around on the altar on the arm of my new husband. I knew how Mama felt, but something else caught my eye. It was a certain gentle unique gleam that I had never before seen in my grandfather's eyes. It expressed the love, the pride, the emotion, the approval that he never was able to put into words. I can't even find the words to express how beautiful and special that brief moment was. And I looked up just in time to catch it. When my eyes traveled to my grandmother's, that look was there too. It was as if I had been their own special child, as though they felt I had done something very good. I'm grateful that I could cherish this one moment with them before I moved away.

I wore many hats during my young adulthood in New Orleans as doors opened, closed and reopened again. For example, I took on the responsibilities of music therapist for the psychiatric wards of Charity Hospital, where I challenged a white guard who did not want me to enter through the front door that was used by all other professionals on the staff. Every day I would defiantly walk as far as I could towards the front entrance before he ran to block my way and make me take the "colored" entrance.

I remember the stares of one husky white janitress who would put her hands on her hips as she watched me go about my work. Despite her refusal to return my greetings as I politely bade her the time of day, despite her protests of my use of the professional women's restroom facilities even though I encountered no resistance from the female psychiatrists, nurses, social workers and other therapists, I offered her only friendliness.

Eventually, I advanced to the position of supervisor of my department, and in time that same janitress would speak to me and even attempt lengthy conversations. Also in time, the guard would stop turning away me and other black professionals from the front entrance.

Later, I became one of the first black teachers selected to join the ranks of the white faculty of the New Orleans public school system. I worked there for many years and gained more lifelong friends among both the faculty and the students.

At one point, however, I summoned the courage to audition for and be accepted as a regular member of the New Orleans Opera Association, one of the first black people to do so. I sang and made many dear friends for seven years. I was never a star, but I fulfilled my lifelong ambition to be a professional opera singer.

The music department of Tulane University actually urged me to study and earn my master's degree there, but as I was making preparations to study at Tulane God took me in a very different direction.

Be careful what you ask of God. He is always listening, He is omnipotent and delivers in His own time, which might be later on but sometimes is right now. All my life, ever since ballet days, I wanted so to go to New York City but never got that opportunity. There was always something preventing me, and it seemed everyone made it to the Big Apple except myself.

At the time, I was a reading teacher at W.L. Cohen High School. The drive from my home in East New Orleans to my work was such a long one and traffic on I-10 was daunting. Having received a summons for jury duty, I presumed that since the courthouse was only half the distance away I'd take a break from the interstate traffic and take more leisurely side streets. The morning I attempted my relaxed drive, however, I found my planned route so unusually jammed that I realized the need to access that dreaded freeway in order to reach my destination in a timely manner. Exasperated as I drove on, I called out, "Oh, God! Can't you fix it so I don't have to drive on this awful I-10 for the rest of my life?"

Once at the courthouse, I found myself chosen for a case. I phoned my husband's work to let him know of my selection and that I had no idea what time I would be home. Mel said, "I've got news for you, too.

I've just been promoted and we have to get ready to move up north in a few weeks." Flabbergasted, I told him what I had asked God just about two hours ago. I then asked him "How far north? Where?" He answered, "Indiana. But we can talk about it when you get home."

Stunned, I hung up the phone and told my fellow jurors what I'd just learned. I then silently prayed that I could contain myself sufficiently to give the case a fair hearing. I had so much to think about now. Though I managed to discipline my attention, one thought that kept hovering over me was the rapidity with which God had answered my prayer.

Driving home, it dawned on me all I'd be leaving behind: lifetime tenure as a teacher, lifelong friends, my mother, my grandparents, the opera, my fellow teachers, my students, Dookie Chase's stuffed crabs, late night fried oyster po' boy sandwiches, and the beignets from Café du Monde. What would this move mean to my own children? I must remain clear-headed to facilitate this huge transition for them.

I loved the little brick house we had on Brevard Street in New Orleans. I hated to put it up for sale. So many happy memories had been made in that home. It was the first house my husband and I had bought. Yet we left it in the hands of realtors as I took time off from work to go search for a new home in Indianapolis.

I hadn't understood yet that I had become a corporate wife. Certain things would be expected of me in that role and my way of life would change as my husband climbed up the corporate ladder. Not all the changes would be to my liking. I understood that I no longer would have to work, but I wanted to continue my own personal development and maintain my own identity. This would not be easy. I knew in my soul that I was an educator and an artist as well as a wife and mother. Through it all, I maintained my independent streak.

Having selected a house, I returned to our home in New Orleans in order to prepare everything for the moving van. I tried to remain optimistic in the process of relocation, but the voices of New Orleans did not want me to go. My opera director warned that there would be no suitable opera venues where we were going—nothing of the caliber I'd enjoyed under his direction. He even urged Mel to let him find other employment for him in New Orleans so we could stay. At least the director knew what opera meant to me. I'm grateful for that. But we had to go.

The assistant principal at Cohen warned me, "You are making the worst mistake of your life. Don't you realize that all northern blacks are sending their resumes south?" I told him I had to go and tried to remain optimistic.

Having done some needed work on my car, an Acadian man I'd never met before warned me, "Yo' husban' told me where y'all goin'. You not gon' like it up dere 'cause 'dem people ain't *friendly!*" I couldn't understand then why everyone seemed so negative about our leaving. I had so much to do, so many details to attend. It couldn't be as bad as everyone was saying. Anyway, what could I do? I had to keep my family together.

After our move, I had a lot to learn. To my dissatisfaction I discovered that each state had different qualifications for teacher certification; not every place was as integrated as New Orleans had become; and not all Catholic churches had the same rules or spirit. In New Orleans you could live wherever you wanted and teach where you were assigned. In New Orleans, Catholic children were not confirmed until about age eleven or twelve. Upon registering at our new church in Indianapolis, we were confronted with the necessity of getting all three of our children confirmed immediately, as Indiana Catholics confirmed their children at a much earlier age. Somehow we managed.

Since I could not get a teaching position in Indianapolis, I enrolled at the city's campus of Indiana University/Purdue University (known as

IUPUI) for one semester. I continued studying voice at Butler University and enrolled in an acting school. Next door to the acting school I discovered a jazz band. This excited me. I decided then and there what I would pursue. I left my name at the Indianapolis Musicians Union and asked for a referral should anyone need a singer.

Dr. Jean Eichelberger Ivey, my music composition and orchestration teacher back at Xavier, had told me I had talent for composing and urged me to write. But I'd not composed a thing since I left her class. Now I had nothing but time, and I decided the time was right to begin composing. I've heard it said that you can't be a good blues or jazz musician until you'd met deep pain. Well, that year of being uprooted from my beloved New Orleans pulled forth the yearnings of a jazz vocalist and composer. I had so very much to cry about.

The first song I wrote was "City of the River." This obviously referred to New Orleans. As I worked on other songs, a phone call came from an independent producer holding a demonstration recording session and wanted to know if I could sight-read music, as he needed someone to help with background vocals. I took the chance. He liked my voice and moved me from the background to solo lead. When he learned I could write music, he asked to see my "City of the River." I felt I was on my way to a new career, but after only one year in Indianapolis my husband was transferred to Milwaukee, Wisconsin.

We bought a home in the suburb of Brown Deer, one block over the Milwaukee city line. I had a feeling we'd be there a while and as a teacher I could always spot the best schools for my children. I liked the quiet neighborhood, our mature apple trees, the birds and the squirrels. The neighbors were friendly. Yet, I could only substitute teach in Brown Deer, because though the student body was integrated the district had not yet decided to hire black teachers. I found I also could not teach in Milwaukee proper because I lived one block out of its district. But then I discovered alternative education and began to teach adults to read.

I continued to write more music and took voice at the Wisconsin Conservatory of Music. Then Grandpa died, and that brought me back to New Orleans for the funeral. After I returned to Wisconsin, the Indianapolis producer asked me to come back to record an album of my songs. I felt it was a gift from my grandfather. The album was entitled "Sorceress." I thought it was good, but it had limited distribution. Recently, I learned my albums are collector's items and people buy them on the web for up to three hundred dollars apiece!

> I learned my albums are collector's items and people buy them on the web for up to three hundred dollars apiece!

Still in Wisconsin, I studied jazz theory privately with the Director of Jazz Studies of the Wisconsin Conservatory. I stopped so I could compose more music, but then decided to study Reading Specialization at Cardinal Stritch College. I had a hunch about how music enables the brain, and my master's thesis dealt with that topic. Though I did continue to sing with Milwaukee jazz bands, I was offered a great teaching and administrative position in an adult school. It gave me the money to produce another LP, which was titled "Think of This." My inspiration still included memories of New Orleans. One song, "Emma," told a story of my own Grand-aunt Emma Lombard of Algiers. The album also included feelings regarding my search for my African heritage. That song was titled "Gi, Kra, Kroo."

I could not believe the attention and cooperation I received on this album. It got much airplay and the Wisconsin Area Music Industry (WAMI) nominated me Jazz Artist of the Year. Some members of the Board told me that the consensus was that I would probably win the following year. But soon my husband was transferred to St. Louis. We bought a home deep in the woods of Wildwood, Missouri, where I began work on this book. Ten years later, having been transferred to California, we bought a home on a tranquil lake near Sacramento where I finally completed it.

Not surprisingly, my musical endeavors had an effect on my three children. I guess you could say the prophecy of my friend from Xavier's music class was right. They all have been gifted musically and in other ways. At one time or another, they each studied at the Wisconsin Conservatory of Music and became professional musicians in their own right. My daughter Pamela, a gifted flautist, graduated from the conservatory and has taught many a student; my son Melvin, a talented trumpeter, played in the famous marching band of the University of Notre Dame and now works at the university; and my youngest son, Gregory, travels the globe as a world-renown professional jazz saxophonist and recording artist.

In the meantime, I began a much deeper spiritual journey to better know God. I even had a mystical experience of the presence of Jesus that convinced me to finish this book and begin writing sacred jazz. Remember I had felt as a child working in the convent chapel that He was waiting for me to do something? In January of 2006, I finally flew to New York City and recorded a hymn with my youngest son. I feel so humble that God has allowed me to experience so many beautiful things. I am overwhelmed by His gracious gifts. Each time He closed a door, He opened yet another one. He allowed me a better view of the many facets of His Light. He allowed my light to rise in darkness.

I had many more paths to follow in my lifetime, and I am not finished yet. They may be the grist for another book someday. Besides composing music for and recording two albums, I earned two master's degrees in separate disciplines and taught at various colleges in the North. My husband Mel and I raised three beautiful children, and they have begun to give us grandchildren. Grandpa died in 1978 and Grandma in 1983. Mama lived until 1987. I never did meet my biological African father, although I was always searching for him. Ironically, I moved to St.

Louis in 1988 and later discovered that he had died in nearby Kansas City only two years earlier.

I always wondered why St. Peter Claver was drawn to take up the cause of black people. Perhaps it seems a silly thing to some, but to me as a young girl seriously searching for direction, role models and identification were important. It was not that I could not emulate him. I did. But I had already sought counsel from saints from Saint Anne, my special patron, to St. Zita. Remember that my church and school patrons were indeed "All Saints." Still, I needed reassurance back then that God saw goodness in people who were the same color as myself, and I finally found it when Saint Martin de Porres was canonized.

I also experienced difficulty understanding why some Americans would get upset when it was suggested that Jesus, a Jew born in Bethlehem and raised in Egypt, might have been anything but European-looking, with a darker complexion than popularly pictured. I remember as a child seeing in a Christmas crèche one black king among the three wise men led to Christ by the star. I wondered how he got through! Then, too, I chanced to learn that Polish people in the United States as well as in Poland love and revere the beautiful Black Madonna. She is pictured in exquisite dark-skin and holding a dark-skinned baby Jesus.

Because I was a singer, I studied the plight of Marian Anderson, blessed with a most beautiful contralto voice but not allowed to sing at the Metropolitan Opera until she was age fifty-nine, her prime already over. What a career she might have had there. Anderson had been able to sing before the crowned heads of Europe for over nineteen years before this country decided to look past her African features and allow themselves to enjoy the beautiful vocal gift she had to share. America cheated itself.

Mistake me not. I love this greatest and most blessed land in the world despite its flaws. But we can, with grace, do better. I will never forget the saints, living and dead, who God put upon my journey to help nourish my light: my family, neighbors, and friends; the Holy Family nuns; All Saints Church; Father Walsh, and countless others not included here but permanently included in my heart and prayers. To the extent that I succeeded, my story is their story. Through such people, the light of God allowed our group from Algiers—people like Jeanne Marie, Rudy, Henry, Harold and me—to rise as far as we did. We accomplished things that nobody we knew while growing up had ever accomplished. That is why I say to you, my brothers and sisters: dare to leave your comfort zones. Continue to reach out, learn, share and grow. If you do, surely your light will rise in darkness.

Afterword

by Sister Jamie T. Phelps, O.P., Ph.D.
Director of the Institute for Black Catholic Studies
Xavier University of Louisiana, New Orleans

Reading Jo Anne Tardy's reflections on growing up resonated with what I have come to know and love about the Black Catholic Community of New Orleans. Central to her journey was the reality of an extended family that embraced blood relatives and fictive kin alike. Identification and inclusion in a community is central to one's identity and is a central value of Black (African and African American) traditional cultures.

Being Catholic is a process of socialization by which a person is introduced to Jesus and the teachings, popular religiosity, beliefs and practices of a community committed to follow the Way of Jesus as interpreted by the traditions of the Catholic Church. Catholic culture is a multicultural reality throughout the world as well as within the United States. Black Catholics are not an anomaly but a legitimate cultural variation of Catholic life, parallel to other cultural members of the Catholic Family who identify as Irish Catholics, German Catholics, Italian Catholics, Polish Catholics, French Catholics, Latino/Hispanic Catholics, etc.

Jo Anne Tardy and her Black Catholic peers were nurtured in a

"Mecca" of Black and Creole Catholicism—New Orleans. Several communities shared the responsibility of nurturing the faith of Catholics of mixed African, French and Native American descent in the midst of New Orleans' segregated caste and racial divisions. The Sisters of the Holy Family, the Sisters of the Blessed Sacrament, St. Mary's Academy, Xavier Preparatory High School, and Xavier University were all institutions initiated by or for Black and/or Creole Catholics who understood that black people are fully human and of equal worth because all humans are loved and gifted by the same God.

Jo Anne Tardy's life and journey is a fruit of this missionary activity and a witness to the reality that all people are created to be intelligent, free and responsible human beings and called to share their talents and gifts with the community. Her memoir reveals that she was and is a woman of deep faith, broad intellect and wisdom, and rich talents. Her faith and gifts have nurtured not only herself, her husband, and her sons and daughter but also succeeding generations who are being touched even now by the lives of her children, who share her faith and love of music as a medium of celebrating life and honoring God.

Jo Anne Tardy's memoir documents the inculturation of religious traditions wherein cultural streams unite and transform one another: the healing traditions arising from African cultural traditions as practiced by her grandpa Manuel; the love of family and community; the Catholic devotion to the communion of saints; the indomitable faith in a God who hears our prayers and acts in our ordinary lives through the presence of family, priests, women and men religious, classmates, and other sacramental agents of God's unconditional love. These constitute key aspects of what we have come to recognize as characteristic of Black Spirituality.

We owe thanks to Jo Anne Tardy and her family, who know and embody their identity as God's image in black. Those who read this book cannot help but recognize that her life is indeed a Light that has risen in the Darkness!

Other Titles in the American Catholic Experience Series

The Spiritual Apprenticeship of a Curious Catholic
By Jerry Hurtubise
San Francisco attorney Jerry Hurtubise explores his childhood and young adulthood in Indiana, Illinois and California in a series of vignettes that are both touching and humorous. He considers how each encounter and event made him the man he is today as he attempts to master the art of faithful living as a Catholic layman. 96-page paperback, $9.95

Watching My Friend Die
The Honest Death of Bob Schwartz
by Mark Hare
Rochester, New York, journalist Mark Hare documents the lingering death of his friend Bob Schwartz—a high school teacher and songwriter—to pancreatic cancer. The story is told within the deeply-held spiritual convictions of both men. Winner of the 2006 Catholic Press Association Book Award in the "Family Life" category. 143-page paperback, $9.95

Living in Ordinary Time
The Letters of Agatha Rossetti Hessley
by MaryEllen O'Brien
Chicago theologian MaryEllen O'Brien uses the letters of Warren, Pennsylvania, laywoman Agatha Rosetti Hessley to explore the years immediately following the Second Vatican Council. Some of the important, yet sometimes humorous, issues that surface include the initial reactions of Catholics to the kiss of peace, lay Bible study, involvement of the laity in church ministry, priests leaving and marrying, nuns discarding their habits, the development of the RCIA, church renewal movements, and even whether or not the new parish church should have kneelers! 96-page paperback, $9.95

Finding My Way in a Grace-Filled World
by William L. Droel
Rochester, New York, native and current Chicago resident Bill Droel, a leader of the National Center for the Laity, tells the story of his experiences of settling in a community of close-knit neighborhoods and parishes on the south side of Chicago. Along the way, he discusses the relationship between Catholicism and politics, modern culture, and religious fundamentalism. 112-page paperback, $9.95